The seduction of

A Missionary's Recollections

Jorge I. Fernández, mxy

Translated from Spanish by Robert A. Duca, Ph.D.

The seduction of

AFRICA

A Missionary´s Recollections

Jorge I. Fernández, mxy

Translated from Spanish by:
Robert A. Duca, Ph.D.

Photographs:
Yarumal Missionaries
Barsaloi visitors

Design and diagrams:
Jorge I. Correa

Printed at:
Lit. Nueva Era Arteimpres Ltda.
Medellín - Colombia

Advance Printing:
Tecnopress S.A.

First edition
February 2003

ISBN: 958-33-4031-6

"Yahweh, you have seduced me and I let myself be seduced.
You have taken me by force and you prevailed."

Jeremiah 20 :7.

"Go therefore and make disciples
of all nations; and behold,
I am with you all days, even unto
the consummation of the world."

Matthew 28 :18-19.

In memory of Carlos Alberto Calderón
my friend and mission companion,
who died and arose again in Africa.

ACKNOWLEDGEMENTS

My best experience in Africa was as part of a team made up of my companions in adventure. A great part of the writings in this book has been the fruit of reflection, dialogue and moments of prayer together with the Missionaries of Yarumal laboring in Kenya and Ethiopia, but more specifically at the mission in Barsaloi, Kenya. I offer my sincere gratitude to my fraternal team.

Thanks also to all my Samburu friends. I have been blessed by being able to share intimately the joy and hope, sadness and anguish of their mysterious culture.

Throughout more than six years, I have shared these wonderful experiences with my family and friends in various parts of the world. I have felt the special encouragement of all my family, and the inspiration of many friends, to disseminate these writings.

Some years ago, Octavio Acevedo, father of an extraordinary family, encouraged me to compile my experiences in the African desert, so that they might be shared by many others. That is how this book came to be, and I thank all of those who have encouraged me to publish it and translate it from Spanish into English. I want to give my thanks especially to Dr. Robert A. Duca, Ph.D. for his support, friendship and generosity. He is the translator of these recollections. I also want to give my thanks to Fr. Donald Doherty, from Maryknoll, and Mr. Paul Bardwell, Director of the Colombo-Americano in Medellín, Colombia, for reading the English Draft and for their valuable suggestions and encouragement.

Finally, I wish to thank the Yarumal Institute of Foreign Missions for having sent me to labor as an evangelizer on the African continent.

May the seduction of Africa affect all of you and accelerate the arrival of the Kingdom.

Ashe Oleng! Many thanks!

Jorge I.

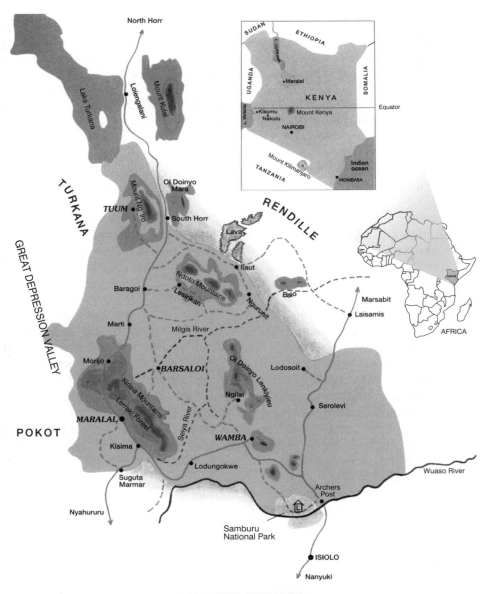

SAMBURU DISTRICT

The most important places where we are present
in Northern Kenya's semi-desert.

THE SEDUCTION OF AFRICA

Ernesto Ochoa Moreno

One reads this book, The Seduction of Africa - A Missionary's Recollections, by Father Jorge Iván Fernández , and senses among its pages and deeply in one's heart a burgeoning of the aromas of Kenya's Samburu desert, the stillness of African nights, the fervor of evangelizing adventure, solitude and remoteness tempered by prayer; in essence, all of that passionate love for other cultures and other peoples arising from the selfless surrender born of a vocation, a true calling, charisma, a sending off. All of this, and much more, integral to a missionary's life.

A member of the Yarumal Missionary Institute founded by Monsignor Builes whose vision was ahead of its time, Jorge Iván Fernández has shuttled over the obscure paths of the Samburu desert since 1994. His figure is not one of a legendary bearded missionary who in the past awakened numerous, thwarted hopes for a vocation in boys and young men, but rather, that of an ordinary, present-day priest, lacking a halo or heroic pursuits, who almost timidly reveals the powerful seduction felt upon assignment to Africa. His tales of missionary life reveal an uncomplicated, pure style, lacking literary pretension, yet witnessing a deep feeling that, of itself, also seduces.

In addition to providing the reader with exciting tales to be read with interest and pleasure, Jorge Iván succeeds in reviving the missionary chronicle, a non-secular literary genre long considered decadent but which remains important both for planting missionary zeal in future generations as well as providing a precise understanding of new trends in present-day evangelization and current missionology.

The last two sections of the book touch upon, conceptually, this new sense of a mission *ad gentes* (to the people). No longer is evangelization apologetic and domineering, but rather, an inculturation of the Gospel within the context of a joyful, humble presence. It has been transformed from an "exported or imported" Christ to testimony of HIM, lived passionately in the midst of non-believers; a mission of "sowing," rather than of "harvesting."

In this light, Jorge Iván's chronicles can be better understood and appreciated. They are novelistic tales, though not novels-life's experiences, at times poetic, but not mere poetry. They are anthropological and social pieces that go much beyond a simple intellectual preoccupation. In addition, the traditional binomial "action-contemplation," ever-present among Catholicism's missionary preoccupations, is skillfully replaced by the existence of prayer revealed in the author's testimony.

The memory of Fr. Carlos Alberto Calderón, who died in Kenya on Good Friday, 1996, resurfaces in The Seduction of Africa's pages. Jorge Iván witnessed the agony of Carlos Alberto's martyrdom. Those of us who knew the unforgettable priest from the Archdiocese of Medellín , immortalized by the Illakir Foundation of Enkai, are aware that his disappearance was not merely a loss, but rather, a symbol of the harshness of a missionary calling. It remains to be seen what Carlos Alberto's sacrifice meant to the clergy of Medellín and Latin America. His ministry was always one of question and answer, excitement and challenge.

This is a beautiful book by a Colombian missionary seduced by Africa, a forgotten continent, in any event, whose echoes we find in that muddle of intermingled blood, the crossbreeding that identifies us. It is a good book for reliving missionary concerns. In the heart of every Christian there is, or should be, a missionary who simply awaits a sign.

The seduction of

AFRICA

Table of contents   Page No.

Leaving our native environment, abandoning the surroundings in which we have been born and raised, in order to go to the desert where the sand, rocks, savage beasts, and scarcity of water are the distinguishing characteristics, is frightening as well as impressive. Desert stopover about 14 kilometers (9 mi.) from Barsaloi.

In Kenya, the hunting of wild animals is prohibited. There are many parks where the great animals can be observed in their natural habitat. Tourists pay for entry into these beautiful preserves with dollars. One gets the impression that animals are treated better than people in this country.

Part
ONE

THE MISSION TERRACE

he mission terrace is especially enchanting. It is the late afternoon meeting place, when shade and breeze become inseparable companions. It is the place of choice for reading a good book after an active day, or for enjoying the close company of my companions in this adventure. From this mission vantage point I can enjoy the games and songs of the Samburu children surrounding the returning herds at sunset. Innumerable beautifully colored birds flutter around me. Their early evening song mingles with the call of a woman asking her young daughter's help in milking the goat does and female camels already inside the camp. The does bleat and their kids create an uproar which resounds throughout the small village. As I gaze through the multicolored eventide, and my imagination begins to wander, I notice the shadow of a woman from my tribe gliding by, as she travels over the burning, rain-starved earth. Her hands move graciously in their efforts to balance a can of water destined for her humble abode. Evening begins to fall, and I think how great it is to feel at home! Smiling diminutive shepherds and the amusing dance of a shepherdess child summon me to live in this African world, so exquisite and untamed, full of passion and mystery.

From the mission terrace, I also suffer for my people. I see hunger and sickness gripping the weakest of them. Soon a discussion between two women begins to heat up, causing all the neighbors to leave their primitive huts and rush to intercede in order to avoid something unfortunate happening in this cluster of homes.

The star-studded night is quite a spectacle in the Samburu semi-desert. It imparts an impressive sensation of proximity and companionship. From the roof deck I gaze fixedly, along with my companions, at the shower of fleeting stars erupting in the sky as if they were miniscule blessings. It is the time to meet intimately with God our Father, or Nkai, the black god of the Samburu, as he is lovingly referred to at all times.

I enjoy immensely our conversations from the mission terrace! After intoning an evening prayer and then maintaining a period of silence, we share the day's events and the ways in which we have encountered the presence of God among the poor, nature's exuberance, our experiences, and of contact with the Word of God. I see the presence of God, as it envelops many good people and fills us with strength.

Momentarily, the moon begins to break through the horizon. The stars, previously radiant and playful, give way to the imposing, majestic, new light. Night is clothed in enchantment. From the terrace, I can see the hand of God resting on the shaven heads of the Samburu women. They dance and sing praise to Nkai, asking him for children and rain. The elders tell long stories as the aroma of roasting meat totally permeates the air.

The roaring of lions fills me with the enchantment of nights spent in the African village of Barsoloi. It makes me want to let my imagination fly. I am in Africa, where man, nature and God live in intimate communion. It is time to rest, and as I approach my room, I give thanks to *Nkai* for his gift of the mission terrace.

The mission terrace is especially enchanting. It is the late afternoon meeting place, when shade and breeze become inseparable companions.

A Samburu young girl. In the background, Nairobi, Kenya's capital.

THERE IS A REAL AFRICA

I have met many people who harbor a distorted view of Africa. They have garnered it from the media showing only Africa's misery, massacres, dense jungle, desert, the atrocities of Idi Amin Dada in the 1970's, famine in Somalia and Ethiopia. They also linger over the war in Angola, apartheid in South Africa, and Muslim fanaticism in Algeria and the Sudan. But we are unfair to ourselves if we dwell on this "Afro-pessimism."

When we actually set foot on African soil, we find many of these things to be true, but the reality is not as pessimistic as we thought it to be.

The continent's name comes from a Greek expression meaning "without cold." In truth, all climates are present here, from the simmering sunlight of many regions, to the ever-present snows of Mt. Kilimanjaro, Africa's highest mountain. At nighttime in the desert, temperatures fall so low that one must bundle up as in any country with cold-climate.

Africa is, in addition, a multiracial continent. Its black majority is found in sub-Saharan Africa; whites have settled in the South, and Arab immigrants in the North. But Africa's entirety was exploited by the European nations that colonized it. Incredibly, it is described as a land without a history, previous to the arrival of the "white" man, although its past was enormously rich, reaching back many thousands of years.

This continent's legacy consists of three main cultures: Its own, foremost, in all its richness; then Western culture, along with Christianity; and finally, Islam.

There is a shameful gap in Africa between a rich minority and the vast majority of the poor, who barely survive. In its large cities we find modern buildings, five-star hotels, luxurious mansions, and multimillionaire presidents who soon become dictators. Politicians, entrepreneurs, diplomats, and employees of the United Nations and non-governmental organizations, make up an elitist class who lack nothing. And there is also the powerful effect of a booming tourist industry, with all its advantages and disadvantages, as opposed to a mass of people who cannot afford the cost of public transportation to get to work. Meanwhile, thousands of people live without drinking water and electricity. The only clothing they can acquire is second-hand, donated by other countries.

Africa does not consist of a sole reality. It is a conglomeration of fifty-four countries, with a population of over 700,000,000 inhabitants, overcrowded with tribes practicing the most surprising customs, and who must resort to three or four languages or dialects in their daily dealings with others.

Great Cities

In Africa, we find modern, teeming cities. Cairo has more than ten million inhabitants; Lagos, Nigeria, more than thirteen million. Kinshasa, capital of the Democratic Republic of the Congo exceeds eight million. Johannesburg, South Africa, is approaching five million. These are metropolises experiencing the problems of a continent rapidly moving from an agrarian to an urban society.

Nairobi, Dar es Salaam, Harare, Addis Ababa, Luanda, Lusaka, Abidjan and many other cities suffer all the problems of countries where the wealth is in the hands of a few, and where the vast majority of the people live in poverty.

Many African nations endure almost absolute poverty, while others comprise a select group in the process of development, and with considerable economic growth. South Africa, Namibia, and some of the northernmost countries bordering the Mediterranean, are exceptionally well-off.

Contrasts

This continent unveils to us many surprising contrasts:

There is the simplicity of rural life as opposed to the enigmatic ancient pyramids and excessive modern buildings.

We find the oral tradition among many groups of people, contrasting with the written traditions of centuries past.

There is glorious, warlike Africa, alongside a more basic, underdeveloped Africa.

Everywhere both agrarian and urban landscapes emerge.

Countering each other are the elite and the masses, religion and secularism, soldiers and politicians.

Islamic influences, and westernization with its capitalism and globalization, besiege the continent.

At times, the cultures of nomadic animal herders and farmers are at odds with one another.

There is a well known anecdote published by Actualité Religieuse dans le Monde (*Current Religious Issues in the World*, No. 121) in which a universal super-computer is asked to give numbers and statistics regarding Africa, and the reply is: The continent is non-existent. In a similar manner, notice was given by a London newspaper regarding the publication of a new map of the world, updating the entries according to neoliberal economics. In this publication, the sub-Saharan region of the African continent is depicted as an immense void. Only white Africa in the North, rich in tourism, and South Africa, with its promise of still-unexplored riches, appear.

Oscar Arias, winner of the Nobel Peace Prize, remarked at an international forum, "If one day the oceans were to swallow up sub-Saharan Africa, Europe would not take notice, and the United States, even less so."

It is from that Africa, non-existent in their elitist computer as far as the arrogant, rich, and opulent North is concerned, that I choose to share my experiences with friends. I want them to know of the Samburu desert's life and death, happiness and hope, the presence of God in my life and those of the people.

We must first note that the continent continues to be colonized even in the face of independence, as an historian of the University of Kinshasa has written.

In 1885, at the Conference of Berlin, the European powers decided to carve up the African pie, resulting in a number of situations from which Africa still suffers.

Eritrea, in 1993, the last African country to become independent, to this day is undergoing a painful process of ethnic, political, and economic turmoil. The upheaval is spurred by a religious situation in which traditional African religions, Christianity and Islam coexist with difficulty.

Many of the problems surfacing in Africa today, (tendentiously presented to the world by the media the former colonizers control) are shown to be the fault of Africans themselves. In reality, the reasons for ethnic violence, for example, are the result of economic, territorial and demographic organization, or rather, "disorganization," imposed by the Europeans.

Such injustice and inequality resulting from colonization and aggravated by other factors, have given rise to past and present violence in Rwanda, Burundi and other areas (conflicts continue because the arms-producing nations so desire). Dictatorial and tyrannical governments continue to rule as a result of the indulgence of wealthy powers and international banking, especially in Switzerland.

Here are some statistics, which help to describe the reality of this continent:

In 1960 Africa had a population of 275 million inhabitants. Today, there are more than 700 million, increasing at a rapid three percent annual rate.

According to the WHO (World Health Organization) estimates, one of every five Africans would be seropositive in the year 2000. In the great lakes region, (Uganda, Rwanda, Burundi) twenty percent of the adult population is infected with the HIV virus. New statistics indicate that Malawi has the highest incidence of AIDS. Thirty-six out of every hundred inhabitants have the virus. In Kenya, the Ministry of Health reports that fourteen percent of the population is infected, with six hundred dying daily from this horrible disease.

In countries such as Mozambique and Mali, the infant mortality rate is greater than ten percent. Of every one hundred children, eight die of illnesses that could have been prevented by vaccination, including German measles and diphtheria. These figures do not include the million children born with AIDS nor the untold number dying of malaria.

The average public health expenditure per capita is the equivalent of five dollars. In Kenya, Tanzania, Uganda and Zambia, this figure is rarely attained.

One hundred-seventy million Africans are undernourished. Forty million suffer from famine and many others are alive, thanks only to international aid.

Farmable land has in large part been abandoned. Many areas are farmed using archaic methods, and eighty percent with human energy, especially women. Sixteen percent utilize animal power, and a mere four percent, agricultural machinery.

Each year Africa loses 3.6 million hectares (approximately 1,460,000 acres) of forestlands. The remaining timberland is less than twenty percent of Africa's original jungle mass. This destruction is due in large part to the need for wood in daily existence, as electricity is lacking.

In 1994, sixty million Africans were affected by wars in eighteen of fifty-four countries of the continent. There are seven million refugees or displaced persons in Africa.

In 1992, Africa's foreign debt, having doubled in the previous ten years, reached 264 billion dollars, which is more than the gross national product of forty-six of her sub-Saharan states.

Of all the countries with sub-standard per capita annual income (less than five hundred dollars per year) more than two-thirds of them are in the African continent.

"Such is the unaltered reality of this continent; thus, from no other point of view than that of economic and sociological statistics, one could easily fall victim to Afro-pessimistic despair. But in light of faith in Jesus Christ and seen from daily encounters with the people, one cannot help but see that the heart of the African people beats intensely to the rhythm of the tom-tom, dance, music, and joy of life, and not just to the pattern of statistics, problems and hardships. Here, more than elsewhere, on this continent of hope, one experiences deeply the true meaning of Easter, the contrast between life and death.

Even as Africa is seen from the outside in terms of numerical analyses, many are guilty of ignoring the hope to be noticed in small initiatives. The latest synod of African bishops is one of those emerging causes of optimism.

Africa does exist. It exists in order to awaken in each of us and in the human heart, a feeling of solidarity; in order to tell those responsible for the world's economy that it is unjust, that it is a crime of the more prosperous nations to continue economic planning according to the neoliberal death model excluding those who cannot produce nor consume. It exists to inform us that life is stronger than death and that happiness and hope must not succumb to pessimism and pain. It exists to shake up humanity's conscience, as does Jesus' cross. We must be capable of allowing the rhythm of paschal happiness in the Resurrected to reverberate more than the sound of death, pessimism and despair".
(Father Carlos Alberto Calderón).

African enlightenment

The chief stratagem employed during slavery times was to de-Africanize the dispersed slaves by having captives forget their origins as quickly as possible, and thereby reduce the risk of homesickness and the will to escape. Today, we must assess the movement toward re-Africanization existing in Latin America and the Caribbean: Afro-American groups; the underground railroad; cultural revitalization; the adoption of African names, hair styles and clothing; the desire to know one's roots; an appreciation of ancestral customs and traditions; (Today, one fifth of all those of African descent live in the Western Hemisphere. Brazil has the second largest Afro population in the world, after Nigeria, the most populous country of Africa); an evaluation of the spirituality, religious beliefs, and music of Africa's tribes; and continued solidarity of the continent.

Africa has produced geniuses in the fields of science, art, literature, music and research, who are scattered throughout the world. The black race is a noteworthy contributor to the field of sports. Many athletes from poor, underdeveloped countries dominate the world's great sports events by their examples of how to overcome obstacles, their discipline and their physical prowess.

Julius Nyerere, former President of Tanzania, has said, "All blacks looked at themselves in relation to Europeans and discovered that all are but one. Thus was born the African identity. Does a true Africa exist, or does it not?"

14

May Nkai, the God of all, bless us… Nkai
May he send forth his rain… Nkai
and strengthen life… Nkai
May he increase our children… Nkai
and our herds… Nkai
and grant us abundant peace… Nkai

Beautiful women of the Samburu tribe on one of the Tuum mission pathways.

AN AFRICAN CREED *

We believe in the one High God, who out of love created the beautiful world and everything good in it. He created man and wanted man to be happy in the world. God loves the world and every nation and tribe on the earth. We have known this High God in the darkness, and now we know him in the light. God promised in the book of his word, the Bible, that he would save the world and all the nations and tribes.

We believe that God, made good his promise by sending his son, Jesus Christ, a man in the flesh, a Jew by tribe, born poor in a little village, who left his home and was always on safari doing good, curing people by the power of God, teaching about God and man, showing that the meaning of religion is love. He was rejected by his people, tortured and nailed hands and feet to a cross, and died. He lay buried in the grave, but the hyenas did not touch him, and on the third day, he rose from the grave. He ascended to the skies. He is the Lord.

We believe that all our sins are forgiven through him. All who have faith in him must be sorry for their sins, be baptized in the Holy Spirit of God, live the rules of love and share the bread together in love, to announce the good news to others until Jesus comes again. We are waiting for him. He is alive. He lives.

This we believe. Amen.

* Donovan, Vincent J., *Christianity Rediscovered*, 1978 Fides/Claretian Notre Dame, Indiana 46556, p. 200.

A BEGINNER'S VOYAGE

Early in 1982, the Missionaries of Yarumal began to arrive on African soil. They took up residence in both Kenya and Angola. By 1994, I was invited to join a team of Latin American missionaries working in Kenya. Since 1989, I had been working in Buenaventura, a port city on the Pacific coast of Colombia, sharing Jesus' Word with black groups of the region. This experience in "Colombia's Africa," was a happy one, and at the same time it prepared me for the voyage to the *Dark Continent*.

In June of 1994, my companions hastened somewhat my arrival in Kenya since a pastor's position was opening up.

Numerous people still had vivid images of the genocidal massacres in Rwanda and Burundi. Many of my friends and especially the simple people of the port of Buenaventura wept openly, as people had at the time of St. Paul, and warned me not to travel to Africa where I would surely be killed. Others exclaimed, "This is the last time we shall see you. Go with God."

In 1994, the great African Synod in Rome ended. There they had debated important ideas concerning the pronouncement of Christ and the inculturation of the Gospel into the continent where I was to go.

When all the documents had been prepared, June 11th was designated as my departure date. Good-byes are always sad. They are a heady trial, and for a missionary, acquire meaning only if seen in light of one's faith.

At the time, everyone was caught up in the feverish excitement of the soccer World Cup. After a lengthy flight, I arrived in Rome, where I was met by my brother Luis Carlos, himself a Yarumal missionary studying there. After a few days' rest, still recovering from jet lag, I flew with Alitalia, making a stopover at Jedda, Saudi Arabia, and then continued on to Nairobi.

A little before 11:00 PM, I arrived in Kenya, where I was met at the Jomo Kenyatta airport, by a large contingent of Colombian missionaries and a friar from Costa Rica.

The entire trip originating in Colombia took twenty-two hours. Africa welcomed me, and in spite of everything, I felt as if I were very near, yet very far from my homeland. Upon leaving the airport I marveled at the tall buildings and beautiful advertisement displays in the downtown area.

Once at the mission, my fellow companions greeted me with great joy. Our residence is very simple and of limited comfort, but human affability overcomes any physical inconvenience. They had scheduled a meeting of the entire team of Yarumal Missionaries and associated priests working in Kenya. It was a wonderful encounter, with an overwhelming feeling of fraternity among all. I loved the ambiance. This is what I had been hoping for all my life.

I began to brush up on my knowledge of English. Then, for two weeks I was sent to the southern missions, among the Kipsigui tribe, to gain knowledge of the work of my cohorts in the two areas known as Abosi and Longisa. The area is cold but fertile, and the people are very warm-hearted. June, July and August are winter months in Kenya, as the region is overcome with cold waves lowering temperatures considerably. Nairobi, for example, is situated about one thousand six hundred meters (4,800 ft.) above sea level, and during the winter months, the temperature falls below ten degrees centigrade (50$^{\cup}$).

Kenya is located above the equator and experiences all types of climate, yet has no distinct seasons. The cold surprises me for I had always heard people speak of the heat in Africa.

On To Barsaloi

The time has come to leave for the North, in the direction of the semi-desert, toward the imaginary Barsaloi about which many people speak happily and others with fear and trepidation because of the distance and the difficulties encountered. "It is a journey for the strong of heart," as we used to say in the seminary, and I undertake the trip feeling very optimistic. Father Jairo Gómez, our local coordinator, is driving the compact Suzuki. We have left Nairobi around six in the morning and along the way we visit Samburu National Park, where for the first time I get to admire the beautiful, yet fearful, wild animals. During the trip we meet shepherds leading their flocks of camels.

I ask Jairo to wait for me while I take some photographs. He tells me that there are camels everywhere in Barsaloi and says I will end up hating them, as they create traffic jams when travelers are in a hurry. We are about forty kilometers (25 mi.) from Barsaloi. It is ten thirty in the evening and we have come upon the famous Seya River, overflowing with water. Crossing is impossible. My companion warns me of the danger. The river has carried away several vehicles. One evening he had to struggle to save the Suzuki from sand as well as water. "What can we do?" I ask, overtaken with sleep and fatigue. Another option, says Jairo, is to go back the two hundred thirty kilometers (approx. 145 mi.) via Maralal.

I am shocked. The rains falling on the mountain make the river unpredictable. We should have checked the region's weather conditions with the Missionaries of La Consolata laboring in Wamba, a small village on the way to Barsaloi.

My companion says that it is very late and he hates to bother the European missionaries of La Consolata, so it would be better if we continued on our way. I am a little disappointed but I see that Jairo is happy to have "baptized" me in the difficult ways of the region, as he repeated to me the words of the Yarumal Missionaries' founder Builes "Burning zeal, to the point of sacrifice"…

"But when is sacrifice the result of not using our heads?" I ask myself in the middle of the night.

A Very Special Night

We began our long voyage by way of another road and reached another mission directed by African priests. Arriving at Lodongokwe at 1:00 AM, Jairo awakened Father Dominic Lesayon, who greeted us cordially in spite of the late night visit. He served us something to eat and provided us with a place to rest for the night. It was a very small, simple house. After about a half-hour of rest, I heard a vehicle arrive at the mission and someone walking to the area where I was resting. Father Dominic arose saying to his fellow priest, "since it took you so long to get here, I thought you were not going to arrive and I gave your bed to a Colombian priest who is headed for the mission at Barsaloi; so now you will have to sleep on a couch in the living room."

The next morning, as the sun came up, we had to fix a flat tire on our vehicle and then we began the trek to Maralal, the district capital. There, we picked up the mail and after lunch set out on the eighty mile trip to Barsaloi. Along the way we met several people from the tribe. They are a splendid race. Their physical appearance, their smiles, adornments and colorful clothing catch my attention and I am convinced that I shall really enjoy working with these people in such beautiful surroundings. When evening falls we finally arrive at the Barsaloi mission where Fathers Juan Carlos Múnera and Daniel Coral happily await us.

A few adults and many children have arrived to greet us. The circular, fiery sun slowly fades away as the stars begin to shine in the sky. After dinner, we gather on the mission terrace to share our experiences. The roaring of lions, native to the region, interrupts the constant buzzing of insects. Along with young maidens, the warriors sing their beautiful songs; my first night at the mission in Barsaloi seems almost like being in a movie.

Dawn is beautiful. The yellow and black weaver finches are in charge of welcoming me to this new reality with their song. Everything is song, light, sun, nature and life. As I leave the mission and go jogging around the mission grounds many people seem surprised at the presence of this unknown new arrival. I attempt to absorb the new reality and to learn about the people, while my companions help me to mutter my first greetings in the local language.

The insects' nighttime concert is interrupted by the roaring of lions
prevalent in the area close to our Barsaloi mission.

19

FIRST IMPRESSIONS

The mission at Barsaloi, among the Samburu, is an area of Primary Evangelization, the first step toward the acceptance of Jesus Christ. Our order, Missionaries of Yarumal, first arrived there in 1991. It is in the northwestern part of Kenya, not far from Lake Turkana, about five hours drive by way of a sand and stone road. We are more than four hundred kilometers (250 mi.) from Nairobi, Kenya's capital. When drought overcomes this area of semi-desert, many people and animals die.

The traditional culture of the Samburu is exotic and unlike any other human groups we are acquainted with. Men and women decorate themselves considerably, in their favorite color, red. I call this area one of Primary Evangelization, since only a few have heard of Jesus Christ. In many towns, there has never been a baptism, much less the celebration of the Mass. Our faithful consist only of those who have listened to the message, or who timidly approached out of curiosity. Our mission ministers to fifteen villages. In some of them, cars are unknown to the villagers, and when children see a "white man," they become frightened; but if he can greet them in their language, they will come close and want to stroke his hair. They also stare at his hands, as if to say, "He is not one of us."

The Yarumal Missionaries provide the people with health services. And we struggle to maintain life. Our car is the regional ambulance, which we must often use to transport the sick and dying to the nearest hospital, eighty-five kilometers (50 mi.) away. Many times they have died en route; some have given birth in our automobile. When a mother is experiencing complications, we must be ready to depart at any time of the day or evening. The situation often becomes more serious if our car breaks down or gets mired in the sand.

There is hunger in this part of Kenya. From our mission we help to overcome the suffering by distributing concentrated foods to the children, donated by our benefactors.

So that they do not abuse the system, we ask each family to contribute ten shillings, the equivalent of $0.15 US. We also have a work-for-food program. The villagers work at repairing the roads and we repay them with corn and beans to supplement their diet normally consisting of milk, blood, meat and tea. The blood is usually drawn from the jugular vein of their cattle, or saved from an animal being slaughtered. Water here is like gold, for its ever-present yellowish color, as well as for its scarcity throughout the year.

In the mission we have also instituted a water-control program. Though many people come to draw water at the mission well, in some villages they are beginning to build tanks to store water from the two or three months it rains. When we travel, our lunch consists of a cup of tea or a little milk, or whatever else is offered to us along the way. Being conscious of the local reality, how could we consume more food when there is such hunger?

Our coexistence with wild animals

We are required to live with many types of animals here, resulting in a constant state of alertness. People are forced to fortify their huts with thorned branches as protection from the lions roaming about at night. This is the people's way of self-preservation, and also assures the safety of their domestic animals. In spite of all precautions, a leopard or jaguar may jump the fence and devour the young goats. When we travel to neighboring villages, we frequently catch sight of rabbits, gazelles, coyotes, wild boars, hyenas and other minor species of wild animals along the way.

Kenya bans the hunting of wild animals. But there are huge game preserves where the larger animals can be viewed in their natural habitat. The tourists who come here and pay their way with dollars give the impression that in this country animals are more important than people. The ministry in charge of tourism and wild animals will incarcerate anyone convicted of killing a protected animal. At the same time, in the elegant restaurants of Nairobi and Mombasa, both tourists and politicians can enjoy any variety of meat, while the natives who may have suffered a crop failure or themselves have been victims of wild animals rarely receive compensation from the government.

The land produces little or nothing. During the months of rain it becomes green again. There is grazing for the cattle and water is close at hand. The inhabitants of the surrounding area are semi-nomads and the majority of their children do not attend school. The youngsters are entrusted with keeping watch over the family goats from morning to night. Throughout the day, their only food is water (not very "holy"), and a little milk. Youths and adults herd the cows and camels.

Venerable authority

Samburu society is a gerontocracy, where decision-making lies with the elders. All other members of the community - women, the youth and children - can only observe proceedings and must abide by the decisions of the elders. The older a person is, the more he is respected and consulted. This could be a good model for our society, where the elderly, sometimes considered bothersome, are often left out or forgotten. Here the elderly are empowered to issue both blessings and curses, as well as solving the community's problems. Their only clothing is a cloak, most often red in color. They rarely wear ornaments but almost always carry one or two short poles for defense, which also double as a symbol of authority. Slowly, these elders are beginning to understand the importance of educating their children, but at present they send to school only those considered to be of lesser intelligence or less able to tend the herds.

For example, if a family has six children, two will be given an education. The mission supports some schools in the region and has established a nursery where children are fed and cared for. All young children and adolescents attending school learn the two national languages, Kiswahili and English. It is common in much of Africa for the majority of people, with the exception of the elderly, to speak three or more languages.

Men are permitted to marry upon reaching the age of thirty, after having gone through a stage of warrior training that begins with circumcision. Young girls are offered in marriage by their parents who must pay a dowry, usually consisting of seven cows, a young bull, furs and ornaments. Polygamy is widespread among the Samburu. Some men have as many as ten wives. The most obvious reason for this lifestyle is to have an ample workforce watching over the herds, whose size is the measure of Samburu wealth.

When a son is born, the family is presented with a billy goat or a cow by one member of the extended family. Thus, upon reaching adolescence, the male will have his own herd. When a daughter is born, there is no gift-giving.

Houses, called *manyatas*, are so small, an adult can barely stand inside. These huts are constructed of sticks, animal dung, leaves and branches, with a narrow entranceway. A fire is always burning in the *manyata*, where cooking takes place, at times causing an unbearable amount of smoke. There is a corner set aside for the new-born goats. Flies swarm all about.

In the Samburu society people are classified as children (pre-circumcision boys and girls), warriors, and the elders, who are all married men over the age of thirty. A female is circumcised on her wedding day, and is then considered an adult. Some thirteen and fourteen-year old girls already have husbands.

A woman's work consists of building the house, caring for the children, carrying water, preparing food and milking the cattle. The warriors ordinarily dance every evening. Even though they are not permitted to marry, it is acceptable in this culture to have a ten to fifteen year old girlfriend. A young man becomes engaged by gifting his fiancée with beads for her necklaces and ornaments. After the evening dance ritual, it is very common for them to engage in love games and sexual relations. Pregnancy among young, uncircumcised girls is not permitted and is punished in the Samburu culture. This causes frequent abortions, assisted by the girls' mothers, although the elders do not approve.

Not a single book of the Bible has been translated into the Kisamburu language, resulting in the need to translate each Sunday's gospel in preparation for the celebration of the Eucharist or of the Word. When a missionary goes to visit one of the villages, accompanied by a mission nurse, the elders of the tribe congregate and invite the missionary to receive a collective blessing out of gratitude for such a visit. One of the elders intones the blessing and all the others reply, "*Nkai, Nkai*," or "God," in their language. The blessing is received with the missionary's back to the sun, and when the blessing is a solemn one, the elder sprinkles him with milk.

This Is How We Are And How We Live

Five months have passed since Carlos Alberto and I, both members of the mission team, finished our studies of the Kimaasai language in Lemek, land of the Masai, and have now begun our missionary work in Barsaloi. In spite of the physical distance separating us from family and friends we feel close to everyone. We know that following Christ means to place the Kingdom of God above home and family, but not to abandon nor hate them, as some have incorrectly interpreted the words of Luke 14 :25-27.

Our missionary team is comprised of three Missionaries of Yarumal, Juan Carlos Múnera, Jairo Valbuena, and yours truly, along with a priest from the Archdiocese of Medellín, Colombia, Carlos Alberto Calderón, an associate of our Missionary Institute. All four of us are Colombians. Juan Carlos pursued his theological studies here in Kenya and after a year of pastoral work at the mission in Abosi, he was sent to Barsaloi. Jairo did his theological training in Nairobi. Then after a pastoral assignment in Tanzania in order to learn Kiswahili, and in Longisa, with an ethnic group called the Kipsigui, he became part of the missionary team in Barsaloi. Father Carlos Alberto Calderón was the last to join our group. The four of us have initiated an experiment in living and working together, yearning to establish a Christian, evangelical community, as we share all that we are and all that we have.

From the very beginning we realized that the formation of a team was an absolute necessity if we were to sincerely and efficiently undertake our missionary work in this remote corner of the Samburu desert. We aspired to pursue the common goal of introducing Jesus Christ to these semi-nomadic people by uniting our talents and individuality in pursuit of this common goal.

We are located in Northern Kenya, East Africa, relatively near Lake Turkana, famous for its paleontological discoveries. From an ecclesiastical point of view, the mission belongs to the Diocese of Marsabit, and covers an area of approximately 1,200 square kilometers (750 sq. mi.).

This area of the country is extremely arid, though not quite desert, like the Sahara, due to the growth of small bushes. The scarcity of rain makes subsistence agriculture difficult; thus, the people live by herding sheep, goats and camels.

Earning an existence in this way requires that they roam in search of water and pasture land, except during the three rainy months.

By the most common route, Barsaloi is five hundred fifty kilometers (approx. 345 mi.) from Nairobi. There is a shorter route of four hundred eighty kilometers (300 mi.), but through long stretches of treacherous road. Maralal, a commercial center and capital of the Samburu district, is one hundred thirty kilometers (80 mi.) from our place of residence. It is there that we go for our mail and to replenish our food supply. Eighty-five kilometers (50 mi.) away from Barsaloi lies Wamba, a small village where over thirty years ago, in conjunction with the Diocese of Marsabit, an Italian missionary group constructed a large hospital symbolizing the miracle of solidarity. A Latin American writer later was to refer to this as "the kindness of many people." Without this medical center, the vast majority of our people would have died, having been decimated by malaria, polio, parasites or tuberculosis. In these remote areas, medical assistance on the part of the Kenyan government is minimal. Frequently we are called upon to transport people from the surrounding area to the hospital in Wamba, since our Toyota is usually the only vehicle to be found. It is there also that the diocesan pastoral teams are cared for.

As I have stated previously, our mission is a place of Primary Evangelization, where the people experience their first encounter with Jesus Christ, but do not possess a clear vision of the Christian God; therefore, most of them have yet to be baptized.

In the religious communities we prepare small groups of catechumens for baptism, or individuals receiving rudimentary religious instruction. This learning period usually lasts about two years. The rest of the population lives according to its traditional religion, rich in ritual and symbolism worthy of our sincere respect.

Today, the feeling of the Church's missionary workers is not to eradicate and replace, as was done in previous eras, but above all, to share. Today's missionary has succeeded in discovering what San Justino, a saint from the early Christian era, called "the seeds of the Word," or rather, the values God has imparted to all cultures, which are then to be enlightened through the persona of Jesus Christ.

- We began as a team of four missionaries working in Barsaloi, aiming to learn the language, familiarize ourselves with the culture, and prepare the groundwork for a new mission in the same diocese. Since May of 1998, the Missionaries of Yarumal have been sharing the Gospel with the Samburu and Turkana tribes at a mission in Tuum, about one hundred seven kilometers (70 mi) from Barsaloi.

NKAI: THE SAMBURU GOD

Both the Samburu and Masai tribes believe in a divinity they call Nkai or Enkai. In the Maa language, Nkai is a word of feminine gender also used to signify rain, the foundation of life, and survival. But for the Samburu, Nkai is simply the name of God, neither masculine nor feminine in gender, infinite and boundless, an omnipresent force. The God's permanent residence is unknown, but he is thought to be present in marvelous places such as Mount N'giro, a mountain sacred to the Samburu; in a plant; in front of a water fountain; or perceptible on special occasions. Nkai is the god who provides for his people, their source of life and happiness. He is the supreme granter, affectionately called "My Black God." They converse with "Him" as if he were human, treating him with great kindness and turning to him at all times, asking for help or expressing gratitude, seeking his company and protection.

Though the Samburu have no written series of tenets regarding their God, nor even a creed, one can perceive many truths and beliefs regarding Nkai by listening to tribal sayings, proverbs, comments and blessings, most often from the adults, elders or women.

The Samburu are a very religious tribe of believers. The name Nkai forever surfaces in their dialogues and daily activities. Mornings and evenings, the elders gather in a central area of the camp called *Napo*, before an eternal fire, to experience and pray to Nkai. Nkai's name is audible when they first go forth with their herds, when they encounter someone along the way, during gatherings or saying goodbye, and in the evenings before retiring. To be sure, Nkai's name is ever-present in the form of simple prayer.

It can be stated unequivocally that the Samburu believe in one God, one sole being, an article of faith often expressed by the words *Nabo ake Nkai, meatae nkae* (God is but one, there is no other). They have no interceders or saints; prayers are directed to God, with complete trust.

The elders affirm that God-Nkai must be similar to a human being but is somewhat more than one. For example, they say: *Kore Nkai keata nkonyek neata nkiyia amu kedolisho nening'isho* (God has eyes and ears, for he sees and hears). This God is good and merciful, forever caring for his faithful and their flocks, even as the humans sleep. *Llakir*, the stars, are God's caring, protective eyes at night. God also weeps and is compassionate. At times when rain is not forthcoming, but there is a sprinkle or two, the natives say that God is crying over the wickedness and misdeeds of his people. That Nkai is both near and far is expressed by the words, *Kelakua Nkai etaana*.

When a great gathering is held, blessings and prayers to Nkai are usually recited while the people are seated, with heads bowed as a sign of reverence. Some of the elders lead the prayers while others proclaim in unison, "Nkai, Nkai" (God, God), at the same time opening and closing their hands signifying an act of petition or gratitude. Nkai is the grantor of life and death. He is capable of all things, for He is both ever-present and omnipotent. Nkai is God of the universe, both Leader and Savior. He blesses all his beloved with gifts in the form of rain, children and animals. Nkai is a never-ending source *(nkishon nemeiting)* of all forms of life, be they people, animals or things. To possess a multitude of descendants and an abundant flock are signs of his blessing.

Sterility is a terrible disgrace for a Samburu woman. Her husband and the elders will try to remedy the curse through rituals and the sacrifice of an ox, whose melted fat is then sprinkled over the woman's abdomen while the audience chants innumerable prayers to Nkai, petitioning his recognition of and solution to the evil as soon as possible. If the sterile condition persists, boys and girls are then charged with delivering a series of emotional prayers, full of tenderness and simplicity.

If Nkai sends the desired child, it is a time of great happiness. The birth of a son or daughter is cause for celebrating. The Samburu regard offspring as wealth and are also very attentive to their children. (Unlike other tribes who neither kiss nor caress their children in public, the Samburu are very affectionate toward them. Kissing between adults, however, is unheard of.) The day a child is born is celebrated by sacrificing a kid or a billy-goat. Only the women take part and through songs and dances thank Nkai sumptuously as they consume all the meat.

The name Nkai is on the lips of everyone from birth to death. At all great feasts and major reunions blessings abound. The Samburu are a people capable of perceiving God-Nkai in all aspects of life, both good and evil. They pray to Nkai seeking explanations for all of life's experiences, be they comprehensible or incomprehensible.

In the words of the Samburu, *Keas Nkai nayieu na meatae Itung'ani oitore ninye* (God does as he wishes, no human being can rule over Him).

*Young girls from the Turkana tribe in search of water
in the immense semi-desert of Northern Kenya.*

Father Aldo Vetori, a missionary from La Consolata, was the first evangelizer to arrive in Barsaloi, in 1973. The Colombian missionaries, Fathers Jairo Valbuena and Jorge Fernandez, accompany him during the silver anniversary celebration of the mission's founding. The Samburu have presented these missionaries who stopped at Barsaloi, with stoles made of goat skin, a sign of esteem and gratitude.

When has anyone seen in this entire semi-desert a man carrying wood, water, or a child, as women do?
Can there ever be a more dignified life for African women?

perspiration from my face, I asked one of the women to boil a little water for me. The liter of boiled water I brought with me had already been shared with the ailing warrior. In the shade of a beautiful acacia tree, I turned again to contemplate my motorcycle. How much good we could do with some of the many motorcycles found in cities and throughout the countryside. My memory reminded me that in Colombia such vehicles were associated with one's enemies and death. What a pity that so many young people in my home country have no direction in their lives!

On the other hand, out on the limitless plains, upon hearing the thunderous roar of my vehicle, the natives anxiously await with their broad smile, the arrival of both bearers of good fortune, the missionary and the nurse.

The missionary, accompanied by a male nurse is the bearer of good news, happiness and life. How much good could be accomplished with the many motorcycles that exist in cities and their ourskirts!

THE CHURCH-TREE

At our mission in Barsaloi the announcement of Jesus Christ has barely begun. It was only thirty years ago that the first evangelizers began to arrive from time to time. With its fourteen villages, our mission continues to be a starting point of evangelization. Very few people are baptized here, even though we have a large number who come to listen to the Word, as well as some who have taken the preliminary steps toward baptism.

Each day, we missionaries set out to visit the inhabitants of two or three villages, many of which lack a rudimentary chapel. Habitually, when the children hear the arrival of our car or motorcycle they come running to welcome us in search of candy. Then the mothers, adorned with bright and colorful necklaces and bearing small children on their backs, greet us with their broad smiles. They immediately begin to tell us the news of family and herd. Finally, wearing cloaks and carrying canes, the men come out to receive us. Through smiles, greetings and news, we move on to the church-tree.

Our church-tree does not have walls or pews. Neither does it possess a loud speaker nor a carpet, much less a sanctuary. But the church-tree does breathe forth life and happiness everywhere. Under this immense tree some villagers take a seat on the ground while others sing and still others begin to dance. The children clap to the rhythm of traditional songs; musical instruments are non-existent. Each dance is accompanied by guttural sounds and a polyphony of admirable voices. As the people contemplate the vast landscape, the elders give their blessing while the missionary unites with them in prayer to the God of Life, the Good Father and Creator, the God-*Nkai*, or to My Black Father, as the Samburu affectionately call him.

All of them listen attentively to the word of Nkai, The Good Word of Jesus Christ, the Son of Nkai who became one of us and who lives among us. From Him comes all that is good, holy and noble in every culture.

Then, in between songs, the missionary asks the participants questions and discusses concerns they may have regarding Jesus Christ and his message. At the end of the session, one of the elders raises his walking stick and pronounces the blessing. In times of a solemn blessing the elder sprinkles those present with a mixture of milk and water.

31

He prays to Nkai on behalf of the families and their animals, asking also that Nkai bless them with rain, resulting in pasture for the animals, with peace and harmony among all. Then the elder wishes the best for the missionaries, inviting them to return the following week.

The church-tree's shade is also utilized to set up the mobile clinic and hold community meetings where solutions to existing problems and plans for the group's future are discussed. Through all this activity, the tree remains a symbol of life in constant evolution. One can't help but think of the existence of temples, which are barely visible edifices, without vibrant communities living therein, without God's warming presence

The task of Primary Evangelization is a slow process, initiated without the help of previous guidelines and lacking the enthusiasm short-term success ignites. With a non-dogmatic open mind, one must first learn to be there for the local population, listening, remaining silent, praying, denouncing occasionally, and having a pleasurable time. We must spend hours observing in order to discover hidden meaning behind what we see and hear. Knowing the language is not enough. The most difficult challenge is grasping the subtleties. We are forced to immerse ourselves slowly in the language and, especially, the culture in order to discover the deepest roots of the people.

We begin to accomplish this goal through family visits, openness and sincerity with all, gratuitous and disinterested presentation, and respect for their customs and traditions. Thus, through a simple life-style, without pretension, the church-tree's celebrations begin to impart to our African brothers and sisters the essence of Jesus Christ. They can then reaffirm their own self-worth, forge new community relations and develop a Christian faith intrinsic to their lives.

How wonderful it is to celebrate life and discover the beginnings of hope in the church-tree!

How satisfying to begin to appreciate the festive, joyful circumstances of each church-tree meeting!

How great to be able to thank Nkai, my Black God, for the people of this tribe and for the many others whose prayers and support make our missionary presence possible, while we await the growth of a flourishing tree from these seeds of the Word!

The Missionaries of Yarumal team, and associated pastors from Medellín, realizing the task of Primary Evangelization in Kenya and Ethiopia. Since 1982, we have been serving the vast poor and outlying zones of the African continent.

LIFE OR TRADITION: THE GREAT DILEMMA

Sister Beatriz Khasalamna, a native Ugandan, directs the Saint Anthony Health Center at the mission of Abosi, where the Missionaries of Yarumal work among the Kipsigis.

During the three years she has been with us, Sister Beatriz has been able to help numerous people, but has also seen many lose their lives through adherence to old tribal ways.

Not long ago the health center opened its doors to a young woman experiencing early labor pains. In addition to being eight-months pregnant she was gravely ill with malaria. Sister Beatriz had to make a terrible choice between life or tradition. According to tribal custom, an abortion was in order. Otherwise the expectant mother would have to submit to circumcision, running the risk of bleeding to death, for an uncircumcised woman was prohibited from giving birth.

The young lady was hospitalized during her final month of pregnancy and gave birth to a healthy daughter. A few days later the grandmother arrived at the center inquiring about her daughter and was told of the new grandchild. The grandmother was incredulous.

Nevertheless, she insisted the health center surrender her daughter so that she might be circumcised, otherwise the elders would refuse to admit into the tribe a baby born to a child. Sister Beatriz denied the request, knowing full well the risks involved in regard to the new mother.

Later, Sister Beatriz visited the young woman's family exhorting them to take their daughter in and help her. Though somewhat reluctant, the father agreed, but only on the condition that the new mother be circumcised. Seven months after the grandchild's birth, the event took place.

The story has a happy ending. The young woman, ever thankful for the hospital's services, frequently visits Sister at the health center, where they have become fast friends.

The labor of missionaries, both male and female, is to announce the redeeming Good News of Jesus Christ. That includes defending life, over all customs and traditions, for the great gift that it is.

A COMMUNITY THAT PRAYS, ENCOURAGES AND SENDS FORTH

The constant increase in priestly and religious vocations in Africa, and more specifically Kenya, are evidence of a progressively mature Church. This part of the black continent, having been visited by Saint Francis Xavier in 1542, began a process of evangelization in 1889 with the first missionary team's arrival. For various decades the work of spreading the Good News of Jesus Christ among the poorest of Kenya and other countries of Africa has been shared by institutions from the Americas.

The Maryknoll Missionaries led the way, followed by the Missionaries of Guadalupe from Mexico, and since 1982, the Colombian Missionaries of Yarumal.

During my stay in Kenya I witnessed the arrival at our mission of a young Kipsigui tribesman who had decided to begin studying for the priesthood.

Slowly, these new Christians begin to see the meaning and need for their own vocations, in spite of cultural tradition which dictates that men and women should marry at a certain age and produce numerous progeny, highly valued in their society. Nevertheless, youth of both sexes dare to defy ancestral custom and choose to follow Jesus Christ either in the priesthood or the religious life. Behind this awakening of vocations, there surely is the hand of God. It is Jesus Christ calling upon the selected, to go forth and announce his Good News. The God-given grace acts as water germinating the seeds of faith in the sterile, desert lands of this continent.

The calling and sending forth

But how does a Christian community react to the emergence of a vocation in their midst?

The young man or woman, ordinarily from among the parish or a surrounding village, speaks with either the priest or nun, outlining future intentions.

After a while, a parental discussion with the male or female candidate takes place. Initially the parents are reluctant to approve and many times succeed in discouraging their child. The father, thinking of the day his daughter might marry, may have already begun negotiations for her dowry.

Once the parents are in agreement with the son or daughter's decision to prepare for a religious vocation, they communicate the choice to the entire Christian community who in turn promise with great joy to pray and to help sustain the new vocation, as the aspiring priest or nun is sent forth.

Everyone gathers in the main church on the day the candidate must leave, for each village has sent its representatives to the celebration and departure. It is not unusual to find individuals or groups who have walked three hours or more in order to be a part of this important moment for the community. The celebration of the Eucharist is experienced in pure African style and meaning; that is, with song, dance, prayer and offerings. The Mass, with prayers for the special intention of the candidate's vocational perseverance, commonly lasts more than two hours.

At the conclusion of the Eucharistic ceremony, all those attending gather on the green areas of the parish for the purpose of sharing the company of and offering gifts to the seminarian or postulant. Each delegation presents a tribute, usually clothing or money. The recipient carries a basket in which to accept the money; clothing must be measured over the body, to the rhythm of the dancing spectators. Each delegation's representative conveys greetings and prayers from the home community, followed by the promise of a team selected from all groups present, to visit the candidate at least once a year at the place of formative study.

As a gesture of gratitude the seminarian or nun-postulant will spend about a week, as determined by the priest, in the communities which have provided the farewell. Life here truly becomes a manifestation of the faith of a community which **prays**, **supports** and **sends forth** its candidates, while feeling deeply the responsibility to encourage and sustain a vocation that blossomed from its bosom.

In Kenya and many of Africa's communities, vocations depend on the combined effort of all the Christian families belonging to a parish and not solely the support of the candidate's family.

Some of the verses sung by the Kipsigis and translated by one of the Yarumal Missionaries while the people were dancing, are as follows:

"May the Lord bless you and enlighten you so that you may follow him each day. May he grant you agile legs and a powerful voice to travel and proclaim him. Laughter and weeping go side by side, so always proclaim the joy of your salvation by example and testimony, and you shall see that the sad and weak will be strengthened by you."

FEMALE CIRCUMCISION:
WHEN WILL IT CEASE?

A few years ago I was watching a television movie featuring various African customs and traditions, and when they showed the ritual of female circumcision, I thought surely that it had to be something out of the past, another example of film editing meant to shock the viewers.

To my great surprise, as a new arrival at our mission I was invited to a circumcision "feast" where I experienced and even shared the reality of this tradition, all the while learning somewhat the reasons behind the practice and the rationale for continuing to do so.

Charles Leorto is a young man fortunate enough to pursue an education, and who eventually became one of our associates at the mission. Nevertheless, he continues to follow the customs of his tribe; just the hint of a change is enough to frighten him. When his sisters Monica and Damaris were to be circumcised, it was at his invitation that I was able to see the practice first hand.

Traditionally, circumcision is performed on a young maiden's wedding day. But for the few girls attending school, the ritual takes place between the ages of twelve and sixteen, during vacation times. The first step is a talk between parents and daughter, in which she is told to prepare herself for the "feast" to take place upon the arrival of the next full moon.

It is also necessary to acquire the quantities of ocher young females will need for painting and decorating themselves on the day of the ceremony. The ocher is prepared with a red mineral and then mixed with lamb fat. In addition, a substantial amount of tobacco is collected for the adults over the age of thirty and their spouses, who will be coming to the parental home.

There will also be sugar, tea, milk, furs, a garment for the young maiden - of black and navy blue material, traditional colors signifying the solemnity of the occasion - as well as a shaving knife. The sacrifice of at least two kid-goats will provide meat especially for the warriors and the uncircumcised young males. If the family is wealthy, several cows will be slaughtered as well.

The girl's father will then speak with the woman responsible for performing the circumcision in order to agree on the price which can amount to the equivalent of ten dollars. In addition, the ritualist will be presented with meat, tobacco, sugar and tea.

The parents of the girl then prepare an area in their small house where she will remain out of sight while recuperating. This reserved spot, called an *Ipee*, consists of a makeshift bed and a large cowhide stretched over a structure of poles. Members of the clan, neighbors and friends from outlying areas are invited to come and take part in the ceremony.

The day preceding the circumcision, the young girl must fill a gourd from a never- ending source of water, then return home to remain in seclusion.

The ritual

The full moon has arrived, and the clan will determine the starting time. Some hold the ceremony between the hours of six and seven in the morning, others between three and four in the afternoon. If in a previous circumcision a young maiden of the clan has died, the starting time must be changed.

Monica Leorto is a slender young Samburu, well-prepared for the ceremony, though unable to conceal her fear. Very early in the morning, the young girl is shaved bald by her mother. The water from the gourd is then poured over her head and allowed to cascade over her nude body, as a sacred symbol of a new life's beginning. Then she is seated on a fresh cowhide taken from a healthy, solid-colored animal. The cowhide was to have been previously spread before the entrance to the maternal home.

A woman, usually a godmother, aids the young girl and supports her by the shoulders while two others, one at each side, grasp her legs, which must remain apart. The woman performing the ritual then bends down and without the use of anesthesia begins to cut the girl's genitals. During the approximately three minutes the operation lasts, she must not cry out nor complain, for it would be taken as a sign of cowardice and viewed unfavorably in this culture. The wound is cleansed, sometimes with cow urine or milk weakened with water, and in an attempt to stop the bleeding of the mutilated clitoris, lamb fat is applied.

After the circumcision the young girl is taken to her prepared place of recuperation and is given a mixture of blood and cow or goat's milk to drink, the only food she will be allowed for the following three days. Then, she will be able to drink milk and eat lamb fat for several more days. Once the operation is completed the woman in charge of the circumcision laughs openly with the other women in attendance, and when asked why, she comments, "Pain does not kill. We laugh because it is our culture and all of us have gone through this before. She is very beautiful because she is an untainted woman. She is an adult now."

While Monica endures the intense pain and continues to hemorrhage as a result of the clitorectomy, the men congratulate the father and remain outside the camp. After their daughters have been circumcised, the Leorto parents cover their own shoulders with animal skins they must wear for several days. The women, who had been present at the surgery, leave the campsite and mingle with the numerous guests.

The warriors begin to arrive from various locations in groups, decorated with all their necklaces, painted and carefully groomed. The songs and dances begin after four o'clock in the afternoon. Minutes later the little girls and adolescent females responsible for tending to the herds appear. This is a chore which keeps them from attending school. They are wearing their necklaces over necks and breasts colored with ochre. The feasting will last until nighttime.

Then the warriors and youthful shepherdesses retire to a grove to partake of the young goat prepared for the feast. It is taboo for warriors to eat meat or other food in the presence of circumcised females, including their own mothers.

The celebration will last two days, with the main dance on the circumcision day. Warriors and their sweethearts dance and sing in a variety of ways. With a special dance, they wend their way to the outer edge of the house where the circumcised female lies. They all serenade her and beg her to come forth to share in the communal happiness, for she is now an adult, ready for someone to win with a dowry. Or perhaps, to bid her goodbye, if her promised one is waiting outside.

A dehumanizing tradition

In spite of condemnation by many humanitarian organizations, and even though prohibited by the Kenyan government, the practice of female circumcision continues. In the meantime, many of us ask ourselves: "Why? And for how long?" The reply is deeply rooted in the culture of these groups. Tradition remains the practice's principal justification.

Samburu, Masai, Kalenjin and other tribes circumcise young girls during puberty by means of an initiation ceremony. Some heavily Muslim-influenced tribes perform female circumcision at the age of seven. Within those tribes who practice it during puberty, circumcision is considered to be the most significant ritual toward adulthood for a woman. In the case of males, circumcision between the ages of twelve and sixteen begins the warrior or *murranazgo* period of their lives. Men are considered adults only when approaching the age of thirty, a time for marriage. Circumcision is an event which ennobles the tribe and strengthens social unity. It also increases the marriage possibilities for a young woman as well as the social status of her father.

The young circumcised woman benefits from the gifts of cattle offered by members of her clan, neighbors and friends, especially since cattle among these semi-nomadic tribes - Samburu-Masai - signify riches, prestige and power.

Suffering and sorrow

According to the World Health Organization, at least ten million women in twenty-six African countries have had to pay a high price for being female. In Kenya, for example, of the twenty-six tribes in existence, twelve practice some form of feminine mutilation.

The W H O also states that circumcision makes childbirth more difficult because of the resultant reduction of the size of the vaginal canal. Moreover it lessens the ability to enjoy sex by suppressing the clitoris; the lesions resulting from this act of mutilation cause psychological as well as physical damage.

In some cases, quite a number of young women have died from hemorrhaging or the contraction of disease. As outlined in various medical reports, frequently recurring complications are urinary-tract infection, chronic vaginal infection, excessive scarring, the growth of stones in the urethra and bladder caused by the obstruction of menstrual flow, followed by infections of the reproductive organs, and infertility. All of this has profound repercussions on the majority of African tribes due to the high mortality rate.

A woman is admired and respected for the number of children she has; sterility is considered a curse. Tribal prayer for a sterile woman is fervid, and draws large numbers of participants.

It is a taboo of serious consequences for a young woman to become pregnant before being circumcised. In such instances, many undergo abortions, carried out by their own mothers. But if the pregnant woman refuses to go along with this custom or it is ineffective due to primitive means, she is expelled from the tribe and in extreme cases can be assassinated to avoid the ridicule of the entire clan. Uncircumcised young women are still children and unable to become mothers according to tribal belief.

Many women admit the practice is dangerous for their daughters but insist they can do nothing to stop it, as the only authority to do so lies with the ruling tribal elders. Female genital mutilation is not new, for the practice goes back to ancient Egyptian times. It was also performed in England and the United States in the 1940's and 1950's to combat hysteria, lesbianism, masturbation and other so-called female abnormalities.

In some tribes men believe circumcision reduces female sexual desire, and thus deters a wife from seeking extramarital relations. Men also believe all uncircumcised young women are undisciplined and promiscuous. According to the elders, a man who weds an uncircumcised female will lose all equilibrium in his marriage and in his home as well.

Teachers of both sexes in the region are worried by the increasing number of circumcised young women who abandon their studies each year, once their fathers have accepted a dowry and set a marriage date for them. Other young girls drop out of school after having been circumcised because of an early pregnancy. "A woman is free to have sexual relations with any man after circumcision and men take advantage of this. It is not part of our culture for a circumcised woman to change a man easily," says James Lekiyai, principal of the primary school in Opiroi, a Samburu district village.

In many tribes, it is inconceivable for a man to marry an uncircumcised woman and a woman, an uncircumcised male. Among the educated, women submit to circumcision knowing full well that it is a harmful practice, though in some tribes young women are rebelling against the custom. As a result, elders will not perform the marriage ceremony for them, and sadly enough, they are classified as minors for the rest of their lives.

Little girls and young women who die before being circumcised, and are therefore childless, do not receive a family burial. Traditionally, their bodies, as well as those of deceased warriors are left to be devoured by hyenas, and lost to the memory of the entire group.

"I never felt anything different, only extreme sorrow; they left me with many expectations, but I was deceived," says Bernardeta Leakayo, a fourteen-year old student at the Santa Maria de Maralal boarding school, who was called upon by her parents to submit to circumcision, as she was already an adolescent. "At first I became very angry at my parents, because it was very painful and I bled a lot; but what more can I do? This is my culture, and the elders rule." Bernardeta adds that she can still recall the pain quite vividly. "Then I decided that I would never circumcise my daughters."

Circumcision and evangelization

From the early days of Christianity until today, the relationship between the liberating message of Jesus Christ and traditional practices, has been one of controversy.

At the time of the apostles, there was much discussion, and the first meeting of Peter and Paul in Jerusalem dealt with the problem of circumcision as one of its central themes. Saint Paul argued against the practice, stating that those who were baptized in Christ needed no other sign; baptism was sufficient.

This was one of Christianity's innovations, an invitation to go beyond the law and accept Christ's offer of salvation (Acts 15 :1-35: Galatians 2 :1-14). The Hebrews argued that one could only attain the Kingdom of God with all rights and privileges by being a descendent of Abraham or by submitting to circumcision to become a member of the chosen people.

The conclusion reached was that God is without a doubt the God of the Gentiles as well. He is the Savior of all mankind: Jews and Greeks, slaves and free men, as Paul states in his letter to the Galatians (3 :28).

In areas where the Catholic Church has a presence, it is ever mindful of the traditions of the local inhabitants and has not officially condemned masculine or feminine circumcision. And in respect to the study of anthropology, an understanding of diverse cultures is indispensable to the missionary. Nevertheless the majority of Catholics worldwide oppose the practice of circumcision, especially in the case of women, which they see as an affront to female dignity.

Through patient dialogue, the situation is changing; education is the key element of this change. As for male circumcision, it has been proven from a medical point of view to have some advantages. Nevertheless, in African circumcision ceremonies conditions of sanitation leave much to be desired. The same knife can be used to circumcise hundreds of young men, and in these times of infectious diseases such as AIDS, there is a real threat of death. To counter the danger, we have tried to provide information to educate those who are in charge of the operation, and also, the young. In the mission dispensary we provide a scalpel for each young person and an antibiotic to avoid infection.

Circumcision is still the most important ceremony in the life of a Samburu male. It is a test of bravery for the young man, who must refrain from shouting or showing any sign of fear during the proceedings, so as not to bring dishonor to his family.

But in the case of females, the initiation ceremony is distinct from that of circumcision. In many tribes, the former is practiced, while the latter is not customary

It will surely be many years before the practice of female circumcision disappears from these tribes. But for the moment the entire Samburu tribe, men and women with whom I live, continue this traditional ritual.

Who really takes an interest in these poor, marginal people? In the face of the government's inability to press for feminine dignity, the Church and some NGOs have the huge responsibility of promoting and explaining these cultures, with the aim of defending life and human rights.

The United Nations' bureaucrats are experts in publishing documents and disseminating propaganda. And various countries have hosted worldwide conferences about women, most recently in Bejing, China. But will these events have any effect on the governments and the forgotten tribes of women who are degraded and mutilated?

Circumcision is the most important ceremony in the life of a Samburu male. It is proof of bravery on the part of the young man who must not show any sign of fear while undergoing it; otherwise it will bring dishonor to his family.

At times, the lions roam at night, so the people customarily surround their homes with hawthorn branches, and in this way protect both themselves and their cattle. In spite of all precautions, a leopard or jaguar will sometimes jump the fence and devour the young kid-goats.

MY FIRST EASTER
IN THE SEMI-DESERT

During my five years as a priest in Colombia I celebrated Easter with all its activities and popular participation, feeling tremendously tired and often having little time to experience internally the essence of our faith.

My first Easter among the Samburu consisted of being in the company of a small group of Christians, and a few others who were slowly learning about Jesus Christ, in preparation for receiving the sacraments.

During Holy Week, I was able to travel to three small villages with the aid of a teacher and my motorcycle. At each stop, we celebrated the presence and introduction of Jesus Christ, dead and risen again, in accordance with the cultural norms found there. The first step in the introduction process is to learn the culture, customs and traditions of the people, so as not to force on them the celebrations, processions, rosary recitations and popular devotions important to our basic faith, but incomprehensible to these human groups.

There are no traditional palm trees here, as we know them, but the people consider some trees to be sacred, and with their branches, water and milk, the elders invited us to pray as they gave a special, solemn blessing to the entire community. A baptism can be celebrated with water and milk, and therefore is more meaningful to the local people. All of them found the message about the kingdom Jesus was searching for to be interesting.

There were not more than a hundred people in each of the villages, and during the day we visited the Samburu *manyatas*, or small huts, where I experienced the joy of the people hearing greetings in their own language from the mouth of a white man. The *kisamburu* language is difficult to learn and the number of foreigners who speak it can be counted on one's fingers. But learning the vernacular is definitively the best tool to penetrate the heart of a culture and also the best means by which to announce the Gospel to each tribe.

At the beginning of each evening, we gathered in the Samburu camps to pray, sing and share something more about Jesus Christ. The full moon which coincides with the celebration of Holy Week was our constant companion as we traveled, and it also served to distance the abundant wild animals of these regions from us.

A new faith experience

The personal experience of faith and life was very intense for me, while the Easter ceremonies were interesting to them. The elders gathered special small sticks to primitively create fire. It wasn't long before they had a huge bonfire. For this new fire they have a special ceremony which includes blessings, songs and dances in which I, too, participated. I was able to immediately grasp their understanding of the symbolism of fire, in reference to Jesus. He has come to shatter the darkness of sin and to instruct us in the best pathway to God. In the midst of this vastly diverse culture, I experienced the redeeming presence of Jesus, who died and rose again. It seems these local people, in turn, also evangelize us.

A CHRISTIAN, BUT WITH TWO WIVES?

Arap Keter is a venerable old man living in one of the Abosi village missions among the Kipsigis tribe of Kenya. It is a place of Primary Evangelization, but the elderly Arap Keter, in keeping with tribal tradition condoning the practice of polygamy, resided there with his two wives. The first wife, now advanced in years, had been baptized in her youth. She gave birth to several children, presently adults, to the elderly Arap, who were concerned about her health. The second and much younger wife kept having children by old Arap Keter.

For several years Father Jairo Gómez had visited, sharing experiences with the sparse number of Christians and religious instruction attendees from the small African village of Guron-Gurik. Almost from the beginning, the elderly Arap became interested in the missionary's presentations of Jesus Christ's message, actively and happily attempting to take part in the religious community's meetings. Consequently, the members of the community appointed him deliverer of blessings and celebration speaker.

Two years later, the old man expressed to Father Jairo his desire to become a Christian and to receive the sacraments, a request the missionary received with feelings of happiness and sadness, knowing full well that the Church could not baptize a man with two wives.

The religious community joyfully shared old Arap's sincere desire to receive the Christian sacraments of initiation. A son of his, a catechist in one of the communities, urged him to seek a solution with the help of the priest and the entire Christian community.

The elderly Arap continued to actively participate in the life of the community. "I want to be a Christian," he said to the priest. "My first wife is like a sister to me, for we no longer have children together." And the entire community knew that the old man was speaking the truth. Someone suggested that he speak to his first wife about his desire to receive the sacraments. She immediately congratulated him as she urged him on, saying, "I always wanted you to become a Christian. I am pleased with this decision; besides, I consider your other wife to be my daughter." The missionary was quite surprised to hear these words.

Amidst great joy, the elderly Arap Keter and his wife received both baptism and First Communion at the celebration of their nuptial Mass. All present were in agreement, having been aware of the kindness, testimony and rectitude of the aged Arap Keter.

The elderly Lobuk is admired and respected throughout the Samburu region. He lives with several wives, has many children and wishes to have more, in order to ensure the family's survival.

In the middle of January 1995, I went with Carlos to Lemek, in the heart of Masai country to study the Maa language which is very similar to Kisamburu, grammatically. He was extremely happy studying the language and knowing he was able to learn a little more about their culture.

A POLYGAMIST'S FAITH

T he elderly Lobuk, an admired and respected man throughout the Samburu region, lives in Lpusi, a village in our Barsaloi mission.

Though he lives with his six wives and numerous offspring, the old man wants to sire more children in order to assure the survival of his family. In this area, some men manage to have as many as nine wives. This is an advantage in a semi-nomadic tribe where the children, and sometimes the women, are responsible for taking the herds to pasture. The greater the number of cattle, the greater the number of children needed. Consequently, very few of them go to school.

Each week, we visit Lpusi and spend time with the Lobuk family. Along with our male nurse we provide health services as well as celebrate the presence of Christ. The elderly man is an enthusiastic promoter for the community. Our small chapel, constructed with the people's help, is filled mostly with his descendants. "I would like to be baptized and become a Christian, but they tell me I cannot, since I am a polygamist; I want all my children to become Christians," the old man states, before breaking into laughter.

Lobuk encourages and invites all his region's people to actively participate in the celebrations in order to know Jesus, beginning with his wives and children. More and more, the other elders governing the tribe become interested in learning something about the Lord Jesus.

With continued blessings he implores us not to miss the weekly visits to his village, no matter what reason there may be, in order to be able to share the gospel with his extensive family as well as with the remaining members of the Lpusi community.

The continent's bishops, gathered at the African Synod held in Rome during Easter of 1994, extensively reviewed pastoral conditions in this part of the world, and some of them even ventured to propose specific canonical legislation. The African Church fervently hopes their pastors will become more understanding evangelizers in regard to the many well-intentioned people wishing to follow Jesus Christ, though they have lived in the shadow of ancestral tradition.

Will we as Christians be capable of bringing about true and effective inculturation of the Gospel?

HOW NICE THAT ANOTHER ONE IS COMING!

One Sunday afternoon, after having celebrated the Eucharist with a Christian group from one of our villages, I went to visit a certain family whose little hut was very near the central roadway. As I arrived, the mother greeted me warmly. The children were playing with several lambs and she was edging a pelt with beads for her daughter Deina. Her husband was not occupying his usual place.

"Where is your husband?" I asked. Immediately changing her posture and voice, she replied, "My husband went to get himself another wife; he is getting married in another district." - "And you, how do you feel about it?" I asked the young mother. Beaming with happiness and smiling from ear to ear she replied enthusiastically, "How nice, another one is coming! There will soon be two of us." - "Are you really that happy?" - "Of course, can't you see that now I will have someone to help me?" she replied.

After this verbal exchange many thoughts ran through my mind. I thought immediately of the people back home, the tears, anger and fights resulting from a spouse's decision to move in with or marry another partner. I also thought about the many ministers of the Church who throw up their hands in horror at adultery or multiple marriages, to the point of condemning to hell the wayward spouse. Then I asked the children if they were in favor of their father acquiring another wife, and they answered that they would be glad to be able to have more brothers and sisters. The new wife would be a second mother to them. In the face of such familial contentment, I express my congratulations and wish them much future happiness. I promised I would return to meet the *Nkaibartani* (young wife), and to greet our old friend. After saying goodbye with a handshake, I set out for the return trip through dusty paths, astride my old motorcycle.

One might ask, "How do these women live together?" "Do they fight amongst themselves?" "Are they jealous of one another?" "How does the husband manage to devote time to each of them?" "And how do the children adjust to one another?" In truth, as in every family, there are problems. But its amazing to see how in the majority of the cases the wives live in harmony and mutual respect. They help one another and take care of all the children as if they were their own. The first wife assumes priority and has control over the others. It is normal for a man not to seek sexual relations with a pregnant wife, and for some time after she has given birth. For the Samburu, the gift of life is assuredly more important than sexual pleasure. (Along with common beliefs, the practice of clitoral surgery may contribute greatly to this attitude.) Brothers and sisters live bound by blood, without problems or tension. They all share the same father.

What a difference in cultures! Polygamy is normal to this society and men and women live quite naturally by the ancient practice. Though having an extensive family is valued in many of Africa's tribes, there are educated young people beginning to question a common way of life and who choose not to become a second, third, or even sixth, wife. A good number of young female students prefer to become single mothers and for this reason many fathers, citing the influence education has on tribal customs, refuse to educate their daughters.

Marriage between women

There are other tribes in Kenya where non-lesbian marriage between women is accepted. When a woman is sterile, has only daughters, is the mother of few children, outlives her children, or feels old and alone, she can pay for a dowry and acquire a wife. This young wife will be in the service of the woman providing the dowry. If the young wife bears children to the husband of the dowry provider, or to another man she designates, all offspring are claimed by the latter female whose family contributed the money. There are outstanding examples of acceptance, friendship, respect and harmony among such female marriages practiced in certain cultures.

The above examples offer many challenges to the process of evangelization. How can Jesus' message be presented to people who have not yet heard mention of Him?

THE STRONGER SEX IN AFRICA

In my lengthy travels through the semi-desert and other stopovers in Eastern Africa, I have often had the opportunity to make new discoveries while admiring the exotic nature of the immense region. Each new day I marvel at the primitive life of people sharing surprisingly diverse customs, as unforgettable faces and situations become embedded in my mind.

I shall never forget the vision of Nkoitel, a young mother traveling in the company of her husband. We met on a dusty road late one afternoon in May, at the hour when the fiery, circular sun was spreading its final rays.

She was carrying a small boy close to her chest, protectively, while on her back was strapped a large jar of water, and on her head, a bundle of firewood. Could I have referred to her as the weaker sex? In front of her, the husband walked along nonchalantly. I knew, too, that when they arrived at their camp, the wife would also have to milk the cows and prepare the meager family meal.

I stopped to greet Nkoitel and was rewarded with a beautiful, sincere smile that remains with me to this day. I had intentionally greeted her first, though I knew that in their society, the man was to be acknowledged before his wife. The husband had stopped for a moment, and leaning on his walking stick, returned a greeting to my partner, a male nurse, and to me, and asked us for news of his friends, as well as information about their health.

Before taking leave of them, and well aware of their customs, I asked the husband why he didn't help her, at least by carrying the child. Without hesitation, the old man answered: "Where I come from only women carry bundles of wood." And he added, "When have you seen anywhere in this semi-desert a man carrying wood, water, or a child, as women do?" Nkoitel looked at me, repeated her smile, and caressed the child.

We gave them our departure blessings and they headed toward their camp. I started the motorcycle and took off for the mission compound. Later, in speaking to the women filling their jars with water from the mission well, I mentioned the incident of the previous day's trek to Raraiti, and how Nkoitel was loaded down while her husband showed no interest in helping her.

52

Their reply was, "Father, what can we do, if life has always been this way. Men do not carry things. We women must build the houses, care for the children, cook, milk the cows, carry water and wood, and often take the herds out to pasture."

While in many areas of the world women struggle for acceptance and display their ability to lead in society, here, in this marginal society, Jesus' Good Word has barely begun to spread. Human rights are well-kept secrets of bureaucrats and government officials.

A small ray of hope has begun to appear as a few Christian husbands begin to set an example for the other men of the tribe. Is it possible that Nkoitel will enjoy a more respected life in the future?

Elizabeth Lititiya comes to meet us and greets us with her beautiful, fresh and unmistakable smile that celebrates one to live the enjoyment of the simple pleasures of life.

FATHER, WHY DON'T YOU MARRY MY DAUGHTER?

The traditional Samburu wedding celebration is full of signs and symbols, joy and local color, songs, dances, food and blessings. It is one of tribal life's most important moments.

The marriage ritual begins with the sacrifice of a young bull on behalf of the groom in front of the bride's parents' home. Four pieces of the animal's flesh are a sign of the couple's pending union. The prospective groom gathers up the meat and carries it into the small hut where his bride is waiting, adorned with numerous necklaces. Her female attendants accept the meat as an appropriate token of the union.

Then the elders of the tribe impart their blessings and those in attendance partake of the meal. Later, the warriors dance with the young females of the group, and in a second gathering the married men do likewise as they sing along with the women of the tribe. Both groups invite me to share in the general happiness.

Painted with a reddish ocher and adorned with all their necklaces, the women show their beauty as queens of the semi-desert. Well-sculpted physical features, perfect teeth and femininity are reflected in their natural, elegant bearing.

Soon, an elder approaches me, takes my hand in a gesture of friendship, and states that he has something important to discuss with me. We go off to the side, where, under the shade of a tree, he asks very sincerely, "Father, why don't you marry my daughter? In the midst of a polygamous people, it is not good for you to be alone, Father." Jokingly, I state that I would readily accept her as a gift, since I have no herd of animals with which to pay the dowry. He then asks if I could perhaps come up with some money. I reply that I have no money either, and am at the mission on a salary. - "Then what do you possess?" I add that I have a head, two eyes, hands and a mouth... The old man smiles and tells me that we aren't likely to reach an agreement.

I then attempt to explain to him why we priests remain single. If I had been looking to marry, I would have stayed behind in my own country, and I would not have come to spend my life with them in order to spread the Good Word of Jesus.

He could not grasp the concept. Among many African tribes a lone, childless man is considered to be a child; he is refuting the gift of life and offends God. Even the mentally ill and deformed have the right to marry and sire children.

Nevertheless, days later when I accompanied the old man in prayer, and we departed to take his ill son to the hospital, he said to me: "May the good God Nkai bless you. Remain with us so that you can teach us to know Jesus, even if you don't get married."

A celibate, given this gift by God, and happily living the community life, is a sign of the work of the Holy Spirit among believers. Somehow the African Church is beginning to become aware of this grace, though it is not yet very clear in their cultural configuration.

"May the good God-Nkai bless you. Remain with us so that you may teach us to know Jesus, even if you don't get married."

WHY DID THEY KILL NASIEKU?

Nasieku was a gracious child, privileged to be able to attend school. During vacation time she was expected to take her father's herd to pasture, and had spent many an evening singing along with the young shepherdesses of neighboring camps. There were eighteen boys and two girls in her class. Nasieku had completed her eighth year of primary education and would tell her father that she wanted to continue studying. Though not entirely in agreement, he sold several animals from his flock to pay for her secondary school tuition. At the mission, we also helped.

Whenever we explained the importance of an education, some of the elders would say, "Who will take care of our herds if we send our children to school?" After two years of secondary school, Nasieku confided to me that she was pregnant and was living with one of the teachers from the school. She was not in favor of having an abortion as many young shepherdesses did, with their mothers' help. The teacher acknowledged he was the father of the child-to-be and stated he wished to marry Nasieku.

The news of Nasieku's pregnancy reached her family, and her father, who was the person to make the decisions in such cases, was informed that the teacher wished to marry the elder man's daughter.

Once the initial contacts between families began, negotiations over the dowry stalemated. Meanwhile, Nasieku's time to give birth was drawing near and her future mate was awaiting word from her father. In the end, no agreement was reached, for according to the elders of the clan, the professor's family did not have a good reputation.

Nasieku had not been circumcised and tribal tradition would not permit an uncircumcised female to give birth. I explained the dangers of circumcision during pregnancy to her family and suggested that they wait until later. The father was adamant, for it would have been scandalous to wait.

During full moon, the family prepared for the circumcision feast, though Nasieku was very much afraid, as she was in the final two weeks of pregnancy. But it was impossible for her to defy tribal tradition and her father's orders.

They proceeded to perform the clitorectomy - surgical removal of the clitoris- and in spite of the intense pain, she did not cry. After several hours of her continual bleeding, both Nasieku and the child died. In the midst of the sorrow and incredulity of family members and guests invited to the feast, the news spread rapidly throughout the region. Her body was left in the open, to be devoured by hyenas.

There was no trial or search for those responsible, even though the people realized that the God-Nkai, to whom they prayed asking to be blessed with children, could not have been in agreement with what had happened. For our tribe, Nasieku's death was a sign that life should be valued more than tradition.

Samburu girls from the village of Raraiti. In our tribe, Nasieku's death has been a symbol for valuing life over tradition.

RAIN BRINGS A HOLIDAY

During the months of April and November, the rhythm of life in this arid region changes remarkably, for it is the time of year when the natives anxiously await the arrival of rain. Women make minor repairs to the roofs of their humble huts or purchase a piece of plastic sheeting as protection from the much-desired rains.

After enduring months without rain, the wind seems to gather force as it howls. Dust clouds begin to dissipate as the first drops of water fall from the heavens. And the people reiterate their prayer of thanks to God with the words, *Nkai ai, Nkai ai, ashe oleng*, (My God, My God, thank You very much). The water has returned and the season's showers are the occasion for much rejoicing as people celebrate the Rain Festival. But it is the children who enjoy it most!

Some of them run to the church area, and completely naked, slide over its waterlogged outdoor floor. Others improvise a type of sled for sliding about. Laughter and shouting contribute to the festive air.

With shaven heads, the women run about the region, amidst song, dance and prayer. In very few days succeeding the first showers, everything seems to have changed. And the arid areas show their pleasure with the rain! Grass and flowers grow so rapidly one can almost observe their development. From one moment to the next the entire region has become a sea of violet-colored flowers. On the horizon thousands of butterflies appear to be cotton balls, and massive clouds of insects have risen from the earth. At night the mosquitoes are a menace. Everywhere there is life and motion! The riverbeds of sand, utilized during a great part of the year as roadways where an automobile can travel at almost 100 kph (63 mph) per hour, have become flooded with water and the swollen rivers emit a loud roar similar to that of a huge waterfall. Travel by car or motorcycle becomes a real adventure as the water's fury transforms everything. Though there are pits and crevices everywhere the people are not disturbed by the fact that the former roadways are impassable. They go long distances on foot, overcoming many obstacles with their donkeys and herds. As the entire countryside becomes drenched with water, it is wonderful to experience the miracle of life in this arid region.

The warriors return from far-away places with their flocks and the expectation of reuniting with their families. Where there is rain, there is life. Pastureland will be abundant, cattle will produce rich milk and meat, and people will begin to regain some of the weight lost during the dry months. How great it is to celebrate and appreciate the festival rain brings, the best gift their god Nkai can give them!

The swarms of flies

Rain is yearned for, and anxiously awaited. It is very pleasing to celebrate with these people the festival of rain coinciding often with the Festival of Easter or the Birth of Jesus, in April and December, respectively. All that was dry and apparently without life has been re-born and is in bloom. Families are together again, milk is abundant, throaty shepherds' songs enliven the afternoons and evenings, and it is time for celebrating weddings, circumcisions and traditional rituals. But the verdant, flowering beauty is accompanied by all sorts of insects, and flies become the inseparable companions of not only the animals, but the humans, as well. It is common to find a young boy or girl whose face is surrounded by a swarm of flies. Eye infections spread rapidly. Attempting to enjoy a milk-filled pumpkin in one of the humble huts where the people gather during the rainy season becomes a race to outpace the ever-present flies. Haste and disgust often times result in the drowning of some of them, but a swarm of flies is a common sight in a glass or milk-filled pumpkin. In the mission residence, as we do not yet have cattle, flies are kept away.

It was Leonardo da Vinci who said water was the impetus for life. At the end of his prayer, an old man said to me, "If there is rain, there is life; if there is water we will have pasture-land. If we have pasture our cattle will be fed and if they are well-fed, we will have an abundance of milk, meat and blood. In other words, we will be able to live."

Rain is the manifestation of Nkai's goodness. When dark, saturated clouds appear, it is time to give thanks to Nkai. Rain is a total event, a great festival.

In coordination with the development office of the Diocese of Marsabit, and including various benefactors' support and community participation, we have succeeded in implementing diverse water projects to lengthen the rain festival in this zone. On some of the mission terraces, cisterns for clean water storage have become a reality. In many areas the shortage of water is so acute that in times of drought the problem appears to be insurmountable. If, in fact, the Kenyan government were to support more specific plans for the utilization of rain and underground water sources, the poor would not be dying for lack of water in the new millennium.   At the present time, within the Catholic Church and with other NGOs, we are attempting to provide a ray of hope for the marginalized shepherds, in the face of this country's ineffective, corrupt government.

The rains continue and the women sing joyously.   The water needed in their homes is now available locally.   Thanks to the additional freedom, they are able to spend more time with their families.   Children enjoy delightful games, the elders give thanks to Nkai and warriors chat animatedly around their fires.   The entire family is able to gather and enjoy hot tea prepared with pure goat, cow or camel's milk.   I love to enjoy a cup of hot tea inside one of the small huts, when the rain and cold keep me from returning to the mission center!

When the rains cease, the feared drought returns.   Shepherds take their flocks from place to place in search of water and pasture.   Camels become wealth for desert inhabitants and for those who live in the semi-arid regions, for the beasts can go as long as two weeks without water.   Prayers and supplications to Nkai are abundant, and in concluding, the petitioners spit in their hands; saliva is the offering they give to Nkai.

I could never have imagined semi-desert inhabitants to be capable of drinking such turbid "water."   If the drought is severe, the consumption of cattle blood increases dramatically.

I fully understood the deep meaning of water on an occasion when I visited an aged blind woman in one of the Samburu camps.   When I offered her my hand in greeting several times, she spit into it.   This was the greatest blessing the old woman could bestow on me.   How great it is to be able to discover that water is the symbol of life and of the love of God, the master of life!

It is a shame we often curse rain for ruining an outing, and we never experience the festival of rain!

How wonderful it is, that we are learning to value and protect our forests, and to live in harmony with nature!

Yet, it is sad our rivers and oceans are more contaminated each day, becoming vast repositories of sewage.

Can it be possible that as we destroy our forests, waste and contaminate our water, we shall learn by force to live the festival of rain?
Rain is truly a time to celebrate!

Here water is gold, not only because of the yellowish color it almost always has, but due to its scarcity throughout the year. At the mission we have also developed a water program. In some towns they are encouraging the construction of tanks to take advantage of the water during the two or three rainy months.

AN EXOTIC LITURGY

The Eucharist is central to Christian life; the acclamation of life itself, and the Resurrection; and the reaffirmation of Christ's celebration with the apostles. Through the feeble efforts to make the Gospel's message inherent to African culture, it is perhaps the liturgical-ceremonial aspect providing the guidelines. In many areas, these external features, with great joy and hope inspired by the Resurrected Christ, are of great assistance in celebrating the faith.

Song and dance, both basic to African custom, have become assimilated into liturgical celebrations quite naturally and with a seriousness worthy of imitation. In these areas, one finds multiple dances to accompany the songs throughout the celebration, expressing with the entire body as well as the voice, the praise, supplication, thankful deeds or offerings to God. Choral variation moves the entire community to joyfully celebrate their faith in the presence of the Resurrected Christ, to the pleasing music of the drum and other traditional instruments.

The perception of time in many African tribes is rather distinct from ours. Here, it seems that time is non-existent. Since Sunday is the most appropriate day for community celebrations, people sing, dance, share the Word of God as well as food, without any reference to time. Conversation, companionship, the value of the word and the capacity to listen are intrinsic to celebrations, with little concern for haste.

A danceable Mass - let us not fear the term - can last for several hours, with the swaying, joyful participation of those in attendance.

In a large part of the liturgy the laity, especially women, are conspicuous for their overt participation. The temple, the Christian community and celebrations are the best places for permitting women to brighten the occasion with their perception and concentration. In a culture where male chauvinism rules and women carry the burden of physical labor, yet are bereft of decision making, they are able to find the possibility of self-expression within the Christian community. A sense of the path to the culmination of a Mass, of the rhythmic offertory parade, and the addition of African signs and symbols are gaining ground over the excessively cold and rigid "Romanized" liturgy.

Is it possible for Latin America to learn something from African celebrations of the Mass?

We Latin Americans have become accustomed to long, postulating sermons and off-key music, and have ignored symbolic and expressive language. Thus, we cannot expect those in attendance at Mass to experience joy, human warmth, and even less, the presence of God.

Yarumal missioner, Father David Guzmán
shares with young Turkana girls in Kenya.

UNITED BY LANGUAGE

*L*earning a new language is not easy, for it requires discipline, perseverance, sacrifice, humility, and a large dose of humor.

Upon entering the limits of another culture and encountering a new people, I am forced to accept the challenge of going beyond the tourist stage in order to become part of this new reality. Cardinal Lavigerie, founder of the Missionaries of Africa, required the members of his community to learn the local language within six months, or face committing mortal sin. Those were other times and another mentality, but the need to learn the vernacular is fundamental to the process of evangelization and the inculturation of the Gospel.

"Language is fundamental to penetrating the essence of a culture." In other words, without knowledge of the local language there can be no authentic evangelization. Christ must be introduced in familiar terms, and not in the language of ancient colonizers. Such statements are accepted by many, but unfortunately, practiced by few.

In choosing not to learn the local language, many support the idea that learning the accepted national language will act to accelerate the "nationalization" of aborigines and lead them out of "darkness." It seems that politicians, economists and many intellectuals believe in teaching only the national language. Others, offering "practical" reasons, prefer not to learn the vernacular, citing "the existence of many languages in a region and   learning one of them would be to discriminate against the others."

The truth lies in the fact that many cultural groups have a high rate of illiteracy, where many of the people have never attended school, and consequently, never had the opportunity to learn the accepted language. What is the solution in these rural areas? To force people to communicate in the national language is to contribute to increasing their marginality and poverty, denies them the right to express themselves properly, and facilitates their loss of identity. One must not mistake pastoral endeavors for economic activity; the missionary's task is to introduce ideas, not to encourage commerce.

In many areas the national language is considered to be the language of business. When a local language becomes extinct, its death erases an accumulation of knowledge, the right to be different, and denies much of history.

It's a pity that in the face of widespread globalization, many local languages are dying out with the complicity of those who espouse plurality and cultural understanding.

The missionary who speaks nothing but the national language finds his pastoral work limited to a certain segment of the population. And many will mark him as an elitist whose concern is for the "educated" alone, while the common people will feel neglected and unloved. The missionary will forever depend on a translator who quite often may say only what the people want to hear, or what he thought he understood.

Only those who have dared to follow the course of suffering and loneliness, silence and crisis experienced in learning a language, will be able to delight in the happiness displayed by natives realizing they are truly loved, their culture is valued, and that they are better able to know God through the language of their ancestors. No longer will only the intelligent and "scholarly" surround the missionary; the poor and uncomplicated, country-folk and "illiterates" will be there as well. The result is a strengthening of friendship, a more sincere hospitality, and the multiplication of reciprocal smiles. It is well worth the effort to learn a new language if only to understand the deep meaning of "united by language."

As the Samburu say, "He who does not speak our language, is our enemy."

Boys and young men dance during the circumcision festival in a clearing area of the Barsaloi mission. Father Jorge Fernández and mission colleagues participate in these most important tribal ceremonies.

Painted in a reddish ochre and wearing all their necklaces, they demonstrate their beauty as queens of the semi-desert. Their well-defined features give them a bearing of natural elegance.

THE SAND CHILD

Among the Samburu people, the women work constantly, even when pregnant and knowing that a new son or daughter will soon be arriving. Many African women perform heavy tasks according to the dictates of tribal custom. During pregnancy the woman carries water, firewood, cooks, takes the herds to pasture, cultivates the soil, builds the house and cares for her children as well as those of others.

A young pregnant woman left her home according to custom, carrying a plastic container on her back, on the way to the post-rainy season current of water flowing from the sandy river bed. Just as she was filling the bottle with the sandy water, the moment when she was to give birth arrived. While the warm sand made for quite a comfortable temporary bed, the mother utilized the river water to bathe both herself and the newborn child. Then, with motherly joy and tenderness, she wrapped the child in a flowing cloth that had served her as a dress, nursed the baby, and headed for home carrying the child and the twenty-liter container of water on her back.

News of the birth spread rapidly among the semi-desert shepherds and the name they gave to the child was Lesunyai (the sand child); the mother, they began calling **Ngoto Lesunyai**, (mother of the sand child). A person's name will always suggest something special or descriptive related to the moment of birth.

Some typical examples are:

Lenkoitei, for a boy who was born in transit, and **Nakoitei**, for a girl born in transit.
Nankai, is a daughter of God, or one born during the rain.
Nasieku, is a girl who arrived very suddenly, when least expected.
Lengarri, for a boy born in the mission car, while it was en route to the hospital.
Nanyamal, a girl who caused many problems at the moment of birth.
Lolpaek, a boy born while the family was eating corn.
Naiguana, a girl born at the moment of meeting someone, or at a gathering.

The sand child will always be carried on the mother's back, on route to the nearest housing complex for water, firewood or food. The end result is the establishment of a very close bond between mother and child, full of affection and protectiveness.

Up and down the sandy, dusty roads of the semi-desert, it is almost unheard of to find an adult woman without a child on her back, even though she must walk for days. In the shade of a tree, she prays and sings to the God Nkai, in gratitude for the wondrous gift of a life. The small child, rocked through the mother's constant motion, bears witness to the prayer meetings of women.

Wouldn't it be great if all women had access to more sanitary hospitals and health centers when giving birth to a son or daughter, just as the privileged women in many areas of the world have!

In the meantime, in this poor and marginal area, close to Bethlehem both culturally and geographically, we struggle to provide traditional midwives with training, and to teach mothers elementary medicine from our mobile clinic.

How many sand children will continue to be born while the world remains so disunited?

AN ACCIDENT IN THE DESERT

A short time ago, my mission colleague, John Gilberto Monroy, suffered an unbelievable accident. In this vast Samburu territory there are only two motorcycles, one belonging to the missionaries and the other to the Barsaloi Christian Children's Fund.

John set out for the village of Opiroi with the express purpose of spending some time among the people and for furthering his knowledge of the local language. It was afternoon, when, loaded-up with a few personal belongings, he said good-bye to his team companions. A little after 6:00 PM, Lopus Losike, driver for the C. C. Fund arrived to tell me he had collided with Father John on a certain curve and that the priest could not walk. Realizing such an accident was almost an impossibility, I at first thought I was the object of a joke. But little by little, I became convinced. Losike's motorbike had a twisted handlebar, and in addition, he presented me with the key to John Gilbert's bike as well as some of his clothing and a shoe. Lopus suggested I leave at once to rescue the disabled missionary suffering from an inflamed foot. I immediately thought it could have been a fracture. In response to my question, Losike told me the foot was not bleeding, but I was worried.

I asked my other colleague, Father Edison Vela, to go with Lopus and help John Gilberto. The wounded man's motorbike had been hidden in the weeds to protect it from the long-tailed monkeys and other wild animals that might be considering causing another accident. I left quickly in order to await the three men as far as I could go with the mission car, avoiding the immense ruts in the crude roadway that were eroded by the torrential rains.

I needed to be prepared for the eventuality of a race to the nearest hospital, some eighty-five kilometers (55mi.) away.

The rescue operation lasted well into the night. My companions had gone to the accident site, while I waited behind, surrounded by woodland vermin, and in the midst of an insect concert, under an enormous ceiling of stars visible only in this region of the tropics. I waited and waited, wondering how things were going for them.

A little before nine o'clock, a light appeared, then the sound of two motorcycles. Lopus arrived with John Gilberto. This had been an extremely rare accident! A crash of two motorcycles in this vast area could not have been orchestrated even with the help of a satellite. But here was John Gilberto, with an inflamed foot and bruised arm. If that wasn't enough, the lights on Father Edison's bike went out and he ended up lying in the sand, though not seriously hurt.

On our way back to Barsaloi, driving slowly for lack of adequate lights, we were greeted by an anxious crowd who marveled at the idea of an accident occurring in the middle of nowhere. Then the mission nurse came forth and announced in his knowledgeable way, that there was no fracture, but much rest would be required.

John Gilberto was laid up for several days, but thankfully, he recovered completely and was able to again ride the comfort bearing, sustaining motorcycle, our only lifeline to many of the areas where the most needy people awaited us.

Father John Gilberto recovered completely and again mounted the bike
of life and happiness, the only means of getting to some of the places
where our poorest brothers await us.

FATHER, GET UP, FOR
THE MOON HAS DIED

One night as I lay sleeping someone approached the mission and began to shout, "Father, get up, for it has died! It died, it died!" Somewhat startled and unaware of what was happening, I ran to the window to see who was calling and to find out who had died. Fraught with emotion, this visitor begged me to get up, "for the moon had died." It was about three o'clock in the morning and everywhere children were singing with great feeling. We were experiencing a lunar eclipse, an event full of meaning for the local people.

Lapa means both "moon" and "month," so it is not unusual for people to ask a pregnant woman how many moons remain until she gives birth. Thus, the moon takes on great significance. Days are counted in "moons;" The local people have no names for the days of the week and dates are regulated by the luminosity or phases of the moon. In addition, the moon is central to all celebrations or festivals, becoming the point of reference for moving forward or delaying a festival.

When a lunar eclipse occurs, the people say that it has died. At that moment, all uncircumcised boys and girls are awakened by their parents so that they may sing and pray to the God Nkai, beseeching him to grant new life to the moon. These boys and girls are aware that without the moon's presence, they will never be circumcised and consequently can never reach adulthood and be re-born as responsible, mature members of the tribe.

At the arrival in the West of the new moon, or "the first day of the moon," the Samburu greet it with deep emotion, pronouncing the following words: *Arro lapa uwa idorrop payie aya loodo* (Oh moon, renew thyself in a short while so that I may have more time for sacrifice and religious ceremony). In some regions, an elder sacrifices a lamb in the doorway of his house and bathes it with *nkarrer* (a mixture of water and milk). Then he burns *malmal* (incense) and pieces of cedar bark. Prayers follow these actions to God, thanking him for the new moon and asking him for the gift of life, enabling one to see another new moon.

The Samburu divide their lunar calendar into two sections which permit or deny the possibility of holding celebrations. The first segment is called *Nkibarra e lapa* (The whiteness of the moon) and lasts from the first to the fifteenth day of the

69

moon. These are the proper days, except for the first day, on which to hold any celebration. The Samburu then choose their favorites among the remaining fourteen days according to the following plan: The second lunar night, the fourth, sixth, ninth, tenth, twelfth and fourteenth (called the green moon, or *lonyori*). The thirteenth lunar night is named *ikaded* or end of the whiteness, and the fifteenth lunar night, *lonyokie* or red moon, the equivalent of full moon.

The second period, called *naimin* (darkness) goes from the sixteenth to the thirtieth night. This section is sub-divided into three categories: a) *Soplain*, running from the sixteenth to the nineteenth lunar night and during which few celebrations are permitted; b) *Mugein*, from the twentieth to the twenty-third night when the few celebrations allowed are exclusively for the clans possessing black cattle; and c) *Naro kutuk*, (black mouth) from the twenty-fourth to the thirtieth night during which the Samburu would never hold a celebration for they say: *Keimina lapa*, (the moon is lost). An animal with a black snout can never be sacrificed in any Samburu celebration.

The Samburu do know the names of the stars and planets, and attribute special meanings to them, such as Venus, the morning star; and Jupiter, star of God, etc. The appearance of a comet, or "tailed star," is an omen of bad luck and, they believe, will bring drought or war.

Nkai-God is the Creator and prime mover of all that exists in the firmament. The Samburu believe God conceals the stars during the day in a place known only to Him, and returns them at night. Nkai is also master of all the sun's activity.

It is here in Africa that I have come to know and admire the lunar phases and how the Samburu regard nature, the sun, moon and stars in intimate communion. The absence of electricity in the semi-desert, as well as all "conveniences" and at times, the enslaving apparatuses electricity brings, such as television, has allowed me to appreciate God's planetary gift in this barren part of the world. From the mission terrace, and aided by a good book of astronomy, I have been able to appreciate this wonder. What a pity those more "civilized," busy in many ways, and dazzled by so many lights, are unable to look to heaven and find the Creator there.

THE MIDNIGHT GAME

ince arriving at Barsaloi, I have particularly noticed the young shepherds and shepherdesses who tend to their herds from dawn until sunset.

On my initial trip here, these boys and girls were the first to greet me with beautiful smiles; and they taught me one of my initial utterances in Samburu: *Inchooki seremente*, (Give me candy!). Every time we meet on these inhospitable roads, they repeat that request. Someone has said that the young herders live a continual "Halloween Day" called, "Give me candy," (their version of our "trick or treat!").

Unable to attend school because they must constantly care for the herds, the children rest only when ill, and, of course, have no time for play. Not until night falls are they able to socialize with others their own age. A shepherd or shepherdess who slept or became careless during the day, causing a goat or one of the sheep to become lost, would be punished by the elders. These young people also live a life apart from the Church. From the start, all evangelizing was conducted in Kiswahili, a language foreign to them, the poorest of the marginal groups.

As I began to acquire more of the local language, I increasingly spent time with these little shepherds and shepherdesses, learning the art of animal herding and enjoying the songs and praises dedicated to their flocks, as well as experiencing the tenderness with which they treated each of the animals. I found it to be true that parents entrusted their animals to the brightest children. Those less intelligent, or with physical limitations, could be allowed to attend school.

Typically, the young herders are happy, enjoy contact with their animals and nature, are simple at heart, and quite skilled in singing, reciting tongue-twisters, and guessing riddles.

In time, some of them began to express the desire to attend church, as school children did, and to get to know more about Nkai and Jesus Christ. But not even Sunday was a day of rest in the life of a shepherd.

Then one day, we decided to invite them to sing and pray outside the church in the evening. A large group came, and thus began a celebration we called "shepherds' Friday" (*mpar e lchekuti*). The children clapped their hands and swayed their heads to the music; then in the local language, we would share the Word of God as well as some tribal traditions. We also conversed and prayed aloud. Each week, these boys and girls happily continue participating, inviting also their parents to pray in unison and to give thanks to Jesus Christ, the Good Shepherd par excellence.

"Father, we, too, would like to study and play as school students do," one of them said to me, to the applause of all those present. I replied, "Are you prepared to study evenings?" And the majority agreed to do so, leading us to organize special classes for them. We were amazed at the speed with which they had learned to read and write. During the day they are in the fields, and in the evening, attend classes, at times with great sacrifice.

Moonlit nights hold special enchantment for the Samburu, and the gaiety of adult songs and dances, little girls' games and smiles of the very young, fill the air prior to the shepherd boys' soccer games which can last until midnight. The short ponchos worn during the day cannot withstand the heated give and take on the field, so a large number of the boys prefer playing in the nude, quite naturally.

Poor shepherds, tending their flocks at Bethlehem, were the first to learn of the newborn Christ. And the Lord also reveals here, to these noble-hearted children, how to live with dignity and hope through participation in the Christian community. They now have access to both education and recreation, in the midst of an ancient culture which formerly bound them to a degrading existence.

THE SHEPHERDESS WHO
CONQUERED THE LION

I t is quite common to say that women have been denied dignity in Africa and many other parts of the world. And the reason that they have become resigned to their fate lies in the fact that cultural norms rule it so.

In all matters related to love and matrimony, the violation of their rights is normal for many women. Numerous girls are given in marriage against their will, and others constantly curse their fate, but nothing can be done to change things. Then suddenly, when "a voice is raised, shouting in the desert," a great number of people attempt to extinguish it. A humble shepherdess once faced-off with a lion stalking her and won, to the amazement of her tribal elders. Her name was Yacinta, and she couldn't have been more than fifteen years old. She never attended school, having been engaged in herding animals in her family's camp since the age of three.

Her food consisted of two or three cups of milk, and some blood during times of drought. There might be a dish of cornmeal, a little tea and bits of meat when an animal died or the tribe was holding a celebration. Recreation was mainly dancing on starry or moonlit nights with young, circumcised warriors who considered her part of their property. While her dream is to marry and add many children to the clan, her greatest wish is to be offered in marriage to someone she loves and, hopefully, of the same age.

But tribal tradition rules otherwise, and therein lies the drama of our little shepherdess.

Yacinta's older sister had the privilege of attending elementary school in the village's tiny schoolhouse. But before the end of her last year, she became pregnant and was offered in marriage without her knowledge. Part of the dowry was paid to her father, and for security reasons, during times of tribal unrest, she was sent to a neighboring area where she was introduced to the groom-to-be.

The man who had paid part of the dowry spoke at length to the father of the young girls, finally reaching an agreement. Yacinta, younger sister of the betrothed, would marry him instead. Yacinta was circumcised, and having endured the mutilation's excruciating pain, then acquired the strength to resist continued suffering.

Having seen the petite Yacinta, and hoping to accumulate the rest of the money for the dowry, the future groom traveled to Mombasa, a tourist haven on the Indian Ocean. Many handsome young men, dressed in their best outfits, congregate there, to be procured by European travelers who pay them generously before sometimes infecting them with AIDS. Meanwhile, Yacinta continued dancing and behaving as a child her own age, though according to society it was time to act as an adult.

After an absence of more than a year, the future groom returned from Mombasa hoping to unite with his bride as soon as possible. She had told us many times of her refusal to go with him, as she did not speak Kiswahili, Kenya's national language, and also did not want to leave her family and community.

It was on a Friday that the father chose for her to depart, without even a marriage celebration. The eight-hour trip was to begin early in the morning in order to arrive at Maralal, the Samburu district capital, and secure public transportation. While reciting our morning prayers, we could hear shouting and laments interrupting the customary silence of the region. At that moment, we realized Yacinta had been beaten by both her father and her betrothed for refusing to go with the latter to Mombasa. In spite of her cries, Yacinta was forced to walk for hours, until, at about fifteen kilometers (almost ten miles) from Barsaloi , the man entered a wooded area to do what Cervantes has said, "no one can do for you." At that instant, the young girl felt liberated from the beast, as she called him, and fled among the thorns and acacia trees of the forest.

He returned to her village, explaining what had happened and hoping to find the fugitive at home, but after two days of waiting, realized the shepherdess would not come back to him. On the third day someone reported having seen Yacinta with two young shepherds her own age, on the outskirts of the village. For an adult woman to associate with uncircumcised males is considered a major offense according to tribal custom.

What then can be done about it? The adults armed themselves and roamed the area in search of the fugitives, their rage increasing as they saw proof the three were competing with lions, cheetahs and leopards in stealing animals. Neighboring herds had lost several goats and lambs.

At last, on the sixth night, the three were discovered, asleep in a nearby decaying hut. Tired from their long search, the adults beat them and threatened them with weapons. It was after midnight when the three fugitives were led to the house of one of the guards from the game preserve, where they would have to wait until morning to appear before the council of elders.

74

Early that morning, I went jogging, as I usually did, and met up with three young warriors who happily recounted how they had discovered the fugitives, had physically punished them, and invited me to see where the three captives were being held.

Accompanied by a member of her betrothed's family, Yacinta was warming herself near some hot embers. The two shepherds, Leng'ida and Lmesiron, were nearby, half-naked.

As a police officer was forcing the boys to perform a task, I greeted them and tried to boost their spirits, telling them not to be afraid and that a little later, I would be accompanying them at their hearing with the elders. I also reminded the officer that the shepherds were minors and should not be subject to beatings.

Minors on trial

At nine o'clock in the morning, all the revered elders gathered atop a hill where a metal cross had been erected to commemorate the silver anniversary of missionary arrival to the region. I went also, accompanied by Fathers Edward Yepes and Franklin J. Carpio.

The meeting began with a solemn blessing by one of the elders, where upon the two young boys were asked to come before the tribunal. With visible signs of the beatings on their backs and faces, they sat in the center of a circle formed by the elders and their assistants. The police inspector opened the hearing charging them with animal theft.

He asked the accused the number of goats they had eaten, and the names of the animals' owners. They replied that it was eight, and divulged the owners' names.

Doubting three people could have eaten so many animals in such a brief period of time, the court was informed that seven had been eaten previously, and only one was devoured in Yacinta's company.

The two respectable elders who were the fathers of the boys spoke, asserting that their sons deserved jail sentences for having become more dangerous animals than those in the nearby wilderness, and everyone seemed to agree.

One of the elders explained that the boys were tribal sons and should not be sent away, perhaps even forgiven. The fathers of the accused were asked if they were in favor of making restitution, and amid the uncommon tears of one of the former, promised to reimburse the owners.

When it was my turn to speak, I gave my opinion of the case. I reminded the court that the boys were minors and should not have been beaten nor given a sentence. In accordance with their culture, the theft should be compensated for. But what about Yacinta, who was not present? They had not wanted to touch upon her case. I reminded them that people should not be forced to do anything against their own will, that in violating Yacinta's rights, the elders were responsible, beginning with her father, a former catechist of ours.

There were warning signs of cultural shock from our way of thinking as opposed to theirs, from the Gospel versus tribal tradition. But the meeting ended with a blessing and it was decided Yacinta's case would be resolved within the family. The boys were ordered to perform chores during the day and at nightfall were permitted to return home.

One of the two boys revealed that he had fallen in love with Yacinta and in spite of his having been beaten and flogged, he remained steadfast in his love for the shepherd girl and even if she were to leave for Mombasa, he would follow her there and return her to her homeland.

Yacinta was taken to the camp of her betrothed's family where she was beaten and, people said, her husband struck her in the face with a stick, causing a scar on her left cheek. The family all agreed that she was to leave for Maralal the following morning with several of their members. After eight hours of harsh travel, Yacinta arrived at the Samburu district capital. After resting the night, the following morning she fled from those who had forced her to go where she did not wish to be. For three days, no one heard of her whereabouts and it was rumored in Barsaloi that perhaps she had committed suicide, something unheard of among the Samburu.

On the third day, Yacinta returned to Barsaloi, smiling in triumph. Before returning to her house, she came to the mission where we greeted her with great happiness. While partaking of a cup of tea, she detailed her adventures and explained how she had escaped from the "lion." "I don't want to go to Mombasa even if I must die," she repeated.

A second meeting of the elders resulted in a more reasonable decision and she was told that she would not be forced to return to Mombasa. Yacinta paid for her rights with her blood. Now, other young girls her age do not wish to marry men seventy or more years old, and neither do they choose to become second or third wives. Yacinta has paved the way, and today is cited as an example for many girls and women whose rights are being denied. "The Church has helped me to be free," she declares. "Love is superior to beatings and cultural traditions."

We must continue fighting so that the rights of the weak are not devoured by "the lion" of inhuman customs.

THE SHEPHERDESS LIBERATED FROM THE LION

At the beginning of 1999, we believed the shepherd girl to be free. But a little later, the lion renewed the attack.

Very early one morning Yacinta sought refuge near the mission; hoping to avoid being seen by her pursuers, she sent us a message. She wanted to speak with the missionaries.

We found her, wounded and hungry. Sad and frightened, she recounted to us all that had transpired and how the man to whom she had been betrothed again insisted on forcing her to go to Mombasa.

Weeping openly, and venting her anger, she revealed how this man she did not love had come the previous day, a Sunday afternoon, accompanied by three others, all of whom beat her and nearly hanged her. "Again they insisted I go to Mombasa, something I refuse to do no matter what. I have been hiding all night, and they say they are looking for me to kill me. Unable to return the dowry, my father has told them to do as they please with me."

We offered Yacinta breakfast and discussed how we could help her. This was too much already, and we had to free her by any possible means.

After expressing our support, we begged her to rest a little. Then we took her to the mission dispensary where the male nurse could examine her and report on her physical condition. Just then, they brought in a seriously ill woman and we had to leave immediately for the hospital at Wamba.

Taking advantage of the situation, we decided Yacinta should accompany us and be seen by the doctor, even though she did not need to be hospitalized. It was important to provide her with a different, more restful atmosphere. The next day, in speaking with the doctor and one of the nuns about Yacinta's predicament, we were told that from their many years of experience in the region, they could forsee that the only acceptable solution was to return the dowry that had been paid, freeing the girl from all commitment. "See what you can do, so that someone pays for her," they said.

Upon our return to the mission, several people asked about Yacinta. We replied that she was doing well, and that the doctor could present her case to the court, a human rights tribunal, or to an Episcopal conference in Nairobi, which would then be prejudicial to her pursuers.

The elders convened and heard that the missionaries were planning to take Yacinta's case to court as a last resort. Faced with this reality, the group was divided. The young girl's father approached Fr. Edward in regard to a loan so that the dowry could be returned. The priest agreed, but on condition that the aggressors come to the mission and with witnesses present, sign a document putting an end to the case locally.

The following day, a group of elders appeared at the mission requesting the money and animals Yacinta's family had received as dowry. After a long discussion and amid threats that the case would be taken to court if they did not cease abusing the young shepherd girl, the elders signed the document specifying how the loan would be paid on behalf of the girl's family.

Our little shepherdess was finally free; she had defeated the "lion" of tradition. Although Yacinta had been circumcised, she has rejoined the young girls' group and now sings and dances peacefully. In the evenings, she studies in the school we have established for the shepherding children.

Yacinta wants to continue studying and some day hopes to fight for the rights and freedom of many girls like her. "The day God wants me to marry, I will do it with the man I love, and not with the old man tradition forces on me. I want to be happy and not enslaved." At the mission, we search for ways to help her. She is the symbol of freedom all of us must learn to appreciate.

NKOLIONTO E YESU
(Young Shepherdesses of Jesus)

Nights in Barsaloi could be the quietest in the world if it were not for the sporadic roaring of the lions, or the songs of warriors and shepherds when the moon is shining.

Our community in Barsaloi has a sizable number of Christians participating in liturgical celebrations and other religious events.

Fortified by our presence, they remain alert to the possible attack of evil-doers, and place all their trust in the God of life, whose sign is the sacred mount. Foremost among the group of Christians are the *nkolionto*, who tend to the herds.

Father Frans Mol, who has more than thirty years' experience as a missionary in Africa, describes the *nkolionto* in his dictionary of Masai language and culture in the following way: "At about the age of six, a girl begins her *ntitoisho*, or passage from childhood to puberty. She will remain at home and gradually learn to care for the young sheep and goats corralled in the *nkang*, or camp. As the girl continues to grow, she will begin to accompany other girls and women in securing water from nearby streams and in gathering firewood."

Also at this age, she will begin to adorn herself with the many necklaces given to her by her father as well as warrior friends, cover her body with reddish ocher for certain festivals, and participate in group singing with the *lmurran*, or warriors. This stage of her life will end when she is promised in matrimony.

The favorite form of entertainment for *inkolionto* to enjoy is the *ranyat*, a combination of song and dance without instrumental accompaniment, short verses sung with one's respective choir, along with leaping and the clapping of hands. A *ranyat* takes place late at night, when the climate is more amenable.

These young shepherd girls have felt welcome among us and have found a place within the Church. Most of them speak only Samburu, and to hear our sermons and prayers in their own language makes them feel it is their Church. To further this feeling of belonging, with the help of our catechist, we have given them the opportunity to sing during liturgical celebrations. Every Friday evening we further this feeling of belonging, with the help of our catechist, we have given them the opportunity to sing during liturgical celebrations. Every Friday evening we hold a special religious instruction session for both girl and boy herders, with songs, prayer, the telling of Biblical stories in Samburu, and lastly, comments on the Word of God.

All of this has made them a part of mission life. They now perceive the embracing Church as inviting them to sing to *Lmurrani Kitok*, the Great Warrior, Jesus Christ, or *Nkerai e Nkai*, the Son of God, who gained for them the battle of life over death and has granted them salvation.

During these twenty-five years of evangelization in Barsaloi, we have felt that one of our greatest challenges has been to continue studying the Lokop (Samburu) language and culture in order to present to them a live Jesus Christ, their friend. We have chosen as well, to serve the poorest and most marginalized group of people, which includes the *nkolionto*. They are generally denied an education; given in marriage without their consent, these girls are the first victims of discrimination at an age when children should be granted the right to study. We must also point out that the Samburu continue to practice female circumcision and are reluctant to discontinue this ritual.

Recently, an elder of the tribe, a Catholic, said to me during a discussion of a young girl's forthcoming circumcision, "I am sorry, Father, but we must circumcise our daughters." (Anecdote by Fr. John G. Monroy).

She was an attractive girl who tended to her father's herd and sang at night with the shepherdesses of neighboring camps.

WHEN THE SAMBURU
WISHED TO EXPEL US

I suppose very few of our friends have ever experienced real physical hunger and God forbid they ever be exposed to this cruelty assailing many of the poor worldwide.

In the days preceding Christmas, 1997, many shepherds were destitute, as a result of excessive rain and the theft of their cattle. At our Barsaloi mission, food was scarce and many people were going hungry. In the absence of governmental help, the people came to us, hoping to borrow our car, which served as the mission ambulance, in order to go for a load of food.

But hazardous road conditions and other personal reasons caused us to suggest that they find other solutions to their problem, as the people in nearby villages had done. Food could be transported by donkeys. Though prohibited in Kenya, a few of the protected animals could be slaughtered out of necessity. The reaction of some was so negative, that the people wanted us to abandon the mission in a matter of minutes.

In the afternoon hours of December 16, an unusual gathering of women and children convened along with the usual elders.

Some of them were adamant in declaring we had to leave the mission for denying the people the use of our car. Unfortunately, among the protesters were intoxicated users of *mirra*, a substance similar to the coca leaf, legal in Kenya and widely used in Africa.

After listening to the wailing, complaints, and insults, with the patience of Job, I rose to explain on behalf of our team the reasons why we had taken such an unpopular position.

It seemed our only recourse was to ask for *melet*, or forgiveness. Upon hearing my words, the community was divided, with some elders, women and children open- mouthed in their amazement, and then they voiced their acceptance of my apology. "It was the first time that we had failed the community." In the end, everyone agreed to accept the apology and after a brief conversation expressed their appreciation for us missionaries and asked that we not abandon them. I added that if I, Fr. Jorge, were to go we would all leave for we were a team. To which many replied, "*Mara, apana*," or "no!"

As the meeting ended, one of the most respected of the elders rose, and holding his walking stick high, gave everyone present a solemn, warm-hearted blessing. Then amid laughter and song, they all came to shake our hands, beginning with the women and children. Many of those in attendance began to scold the incriminators and the intoxicated. In later discussions, others admitted that they had been wrong in misjudging us.

With God's help, a truck loaded with food arrived at dawn, an occasion for widespread jubilation. The evangelization process among the poor and marginalized is not always a bed of roses, for conflicts soon arise.

Helder Camara, the Brazilian bishop so dedicated to helping the poor, once said: "When I give food to a poor man, he tells me I am a saint. When I ask him why he is hungry, he replies that I am a communist." In this same way, the groups we support do not always understand the "whys and wherefores" of our work.

In the face of hunger and human suffering we should never condemn anyone if the lack of food produces violence, resentment, hate, anger or countless other sentiments; this is something I can now understand, for the reality a poor man's experiences has been our teacher. It is a shame that many people, especially in wealthy countries, spend so much money on diets to lose weight, all the while disparaging the food they possess in abundance. Others choose to waste or throw away food, feed it to the animals, or throw it into the ocean, in order to keep the market price high.

When will the world's rich and powerful, authors of the neo-liberal market economy, come to understand the hunger of the poor and unemployed, and see that the rejected or non-productive are without hope?

What can be clearly seen in a given moment, and appears to be the best solution, can quickly change. One must review and pray over decisions. In spite of everything there are always doubts lurking; others see the truth clearly from afar, and condemn one of the positions. Together with my mission team, we pray that the good Lord will show us the correct path each day, and guide us in the way of truth.

The Samburu like to call themselves Lokop, that is, "those who love the earth." They are a Nilo-Hamitic tribe who speak the Maa language, commonly called Masai. The origin of the race is rather mysterious. During some fifteen years of their life, Samburu males belong to the warrior class, which begins with the rite of circumcision. Marriage is permitted for men only after the age of thirty.

AIDS: AFRICA'S ATOMIC BOMB

Peter Lekaldero became a tribal warrior the day he was circumcised along with a substantial group of his peers. He was fifteen years old. He then dedicated himself to caring for the family's animals, dancing along with male friends, and with girls younger in age. He traveled throughout the region, adorned with beautiful necklaces, knife at the waist, a lance, arrow and cane. Dressed in a red cloak, he painted himself with ocher for the festivals. His footwear consisted of a pair of sandals carved from an automobile tire. He loved his long, artificial hair, made from tree fiber. His athletic body and fine physical features defined him as a worthy representative of the Samburu race. Along with the majority of the warriors, he appeared to be a proud and happy follower of tribal custom.

One day, discouraged by severe drought conditions and widespread hunger in the semi-desert, he met up with a group of warriors of his generation who were returning from Mombasa, listening to the music on their radios, and proudly sporting articles from the "civilized world," such as watches, rings, casual wear. Dancing for tourists and selling traditional products meant being able to earn a sizable amount of money to help the family, buy animals, and also put aside something with which to pay a dowry upon reaching the marriageable age of thirty. They eagerly described to him their encounters with European women in Mombasa, port city on the Indian Ocean. There, he would be able to view the huge sea or "big puddle," as the locals called it and meet people with very strange customs. Dazzled by all that his friends had recounted, he sold a few animals from his family's herd and left for Maralal to begin the two-day trip to Mombasa. Upon his arrival there, he met up with other warriors of the tribe who received him cordially and gave him assistance. At first, everything was so new to Peter. He could not understand why the white people enjoyed changing color by exposing themselves to the sun. "And why do they change clothes so many times a day?" he asked one of his friends.

An adventure with a white woman

Tourist season was at its height, and within a week, Peter caught the eye of a beautiful young Swiss lady who offered him money, food, marijuana and anything else he wanted, provided he would satisfy her sexual desires during a two-week vacation there. Bored with her affluent life in Switzerland, the young lady wanted the freedom to do as she pleased. Strict customs and close scrutiny in her small European town forced her to rebel against authority. Her female friends had told her that blacks were sexually attractive.

The young lady returned home and Peter was left behind, excited about the riches of the white man in general, and the generosity of the Swiss lady in particular. A week later, he became involved in the same way with a Dutch woman; then, one from France.

Months later, he moved in with an elderly German woman, a wealthy spinster willing to spend as much money as possible on this warrior she considered to be a demigod. One day the elderly woman purchased an automobile and began to travel around the country with her warrior, ending up in Samburu territory where Peter introduced the *mzungu*, (foreign white woman), to his family. She felt life was a movie scenario. She slept on a cow hide, brought beer, tobacco and *mirra*, -a halucinogen- for the elders; everyone was delighted with this *mzungu* who provided them with food, clothing, money and gifts.

After their venture into Samburu territory the elderly German and her demigod decided to return to Mombasa. Some of the tribal elders did not protest when the *mzungu* presented them with gifts, but at a later meeting they decried the fact that the young were changing tribal customs. "We find it unacceptable for these warriors to walk behind an elderly lady who could be their mother or grandmother. In Africa, the woman always walks behind the man; to do otherwise, is unacceptable," according to the wisdom of one of the elders.

A year later

After about a year of co-habitation with Peter, the German woman fell ill and decided to return to her European home. Upon receiving a settlement of money, Peter went home, planning to prepare for the festival in which all the warriors of his generation would be given permission to marry. During this time, he had sexual relations with two adolescent girls. Soon after, Peter turned thirty, but was no longer himself. His once svelte physique was showing signs of a strange illness. Some tribal members gave him a medicinal potion, fearing that he had been under a spell. One morning, three warriors came to the door of the mission requesting the car to take Peter to the hospital.

Gaunt, constantly coughing, and suffering from diarrhea for several days, he was granted a letter of admission to the health center by our male nurse. I drove the young warrior to the hospital where he was immediately admitted and

84

connected to an IV-bottle; then I said good-by and returned to the mission. When I returned to the hospital with another patient two weeks later, they told me that Peter had contracted AIDS. "It would be better for him to remain at home with his family," they said to me at the hospital, so I took him as far as the entrance-way to Nomboroi, where his family lived. I called out to one of his brothers, a catechist of ours who had gone to school, and explained Peter's situation to him, pointing out how he could be of assistance. I also gave him the hospital report and explained the type of care his ill brother would need. In addition, I related how contagious the disease was and suggested he tell his brother not to marry. But my efforts were all in vain. This seemingly-educated brother insisted Peter should marry in order to leave some progeny behind, for "it is not good that a man should die without having sired children."

A traditional wedding

"Tradition is stronger than life," I thought. A month later, Peter was married in a traditional ceremony. His bride was a beautiful young girl from one of our villages. Peter soon fell seriously ill and was taken to the hospital repeatedly. Eleven months later, he died. His body was left in the sand to be devoured by the hyenas. The young widow was given to a polygamist elder where she would remain, and any children born to her would belong to the family. But several months later, the nkaibartani, or recently married childless woman, became ill and soon died. Many tribal members blamed her death on a curse. A few of them understood it to be the scourge of AIDS.

This terrible illness is worse than an atomic bomb in Africa. Many people on this continent have been infected with it, causing thousands to die each day, leaving behind untold numbers of orphans and infected children.

Among the Samburu, a person infected with AIDS will die within two or three years due to the poverty, lack of medicine and general conditions of life. Governments either do not know what to do, or cannot afford to act. Cultural practices such as polygamy, leviration, circumcision, and promiscuity, account for the speed with which this illness spreads. The blacks say it is an illness of the whites. The whites say it comes from the blacks. Both blacks and whites blame it on the long-tailed monkeys and chimpanzees of the Congo. Blacks, whites and chimpanzees declare it to be a laboratory disease designed to control world population. United Nations bureaucrats echo all possible theories, publishing many documents, but never taking action.

A CEREMONY OF PARDON

One day, the tribal elder Lesiamito, a well-known polygamist at Camp Lorora and member of the Lorokucho clan, came to the mission requesting the help of the missionaries. He wanted us to accompany some of the elders to Marti, to participate in peace talks between representatives of two feuding tribes, the Samburu and the Turkana. "And how will you be of assistance?" I asked Lesiamito and some of the elders. They replied that they were short of money at the time, but were willing to contribute twenty-five dollars. After prolonged consideration, they left three spears at the mission with the understanding that the following week all of them would return with the money and reclaim their spears. A few days later, Lesiamito, without the agreed upon amount, arrived to pick up the spears. I refused to surrender them, telling him I had faith in the good word of the elders, who were not children. He then departed in disgust. The following Tuesday, I went to the Lorora to greet the people and to present my lesson to the students of catechism. Lesiamito, who was somewhat intoxicated, began to treat me with disdain and in vulgar terms threatened to have me removed from the camp. His rude behavior was quickly condemned by Lelepaso, another elder, who chided him for not respecting a priest and in addition, asked Lesiamito to be silent, as he was not the owner of the place. While the exchange of words was going on, others present suggested it would be better for me to return to the mission in order to avoid a more serious encounter. As I was leaving, Lesiamito was shouting, "Leave the Lorora and don't ever return. We don't ever want to see you again around here." After mounting my motorcycle, I sped off, accompanied by another elder.

The following day two elders and several women arrived at the mission begging my forgiveness for what had happened. Then they began to tell me what transpired once I left the place. Lesiamoto and Lelepaso argued for more than half an hour, then came to blows, resulting in blood being shed and the discarding of their cloaks during the disagreement. The two elders were even fighting in the nude before women and children. "*Lpadri, ketorrono ena toki atwua lwenet lang,*" ("Father, this is a very bad thing in our culture"). I explained to them that I regretted what had happened and that we now decided not to return there. That afternoon, I shared the details with my mission companions and we all agreed to stay away from the camp until receiving some sign from the elders that they were sorry. We stopped all visits, use of the mobile clinic, and other services to the area. Then we gave the elders back their spears.

Many people came to us begging forgiveness. The mothers claimed that their children were suffering without a clinic; the students of religious instruction steadfastly prayed for the continued teaching of the Word. "We want you to return," they all said.

A major meeting of the elders was held to arrive at a decision on the Lesiamito versus Lelepaso incident. The council of elders decided to reprimand both men, each of whom was to be fined the sacrifice of one pregnant cow. They were to be pardoned the same day and given a blessing anew. One of the elders said to me, "Father, it is very painful for a Samburu to have to kill a pregnant cow."

After the sacrifice in the Lorora, a large group of elders, including Lesiamito and Lelepaso arrived at the mission, inviting all of the Barsaloi missionary team to participate in a ceremony of pardon, and adding the words, "We want you to be with us always, and we ask for your forgiveness."

On Tuesday, the assigned day, we all left for the Lorora where the women greeted us with tribal dances. There was a long prayer of pardon during which the elders invoked Nkai. We too, prayed, and shared our point of view about the incident. Finally, there was a lengthy blessing, a handshake, and the serving of tea to all those present.

Our friendship grew and the natives appreciated more and more the missionaries' presence, telling their compatriots, "Those Colombians are one of us."

A VERY ORIGINAL EASTER

t is the first time Easter is to be celebrated in Kisamburu, the local vernacular. Foremost among the reasons why it had never been done before was the lack of catechistic material. To this day, we still do not have a Bible nor liturgical texts in the language of the people. Previous missionaries would perform almost all of their duties in Kiswahili, which, along with English, comprised the two national languages. They also relied on catechists or translators. In this region, barely ten percent of the people understand a language other than Kisamburu.

Although in previous years efforts were made to conduct Mass in the local language, this was the first time we were able to offer Holy Week services comprehensible to the tribe, aided by the pamphlet publications of the Diocese of Maralal, under whose jurisdiction our mission fell. We must once more emphasize that language is the key to penetrating the heart of a culture, and the way to make progress in the inculturation of the Gospel. We cannot continue to evangelize in the language and manner of colonizers.

In this region of Eastern Africa, we are not far removed from the cultural, social and religious influences of the people of Israel as well as that of the Nilotic peoples of Northern Africa, such as the Egyptians, Ethiopians, etc., to whom the Samburu and many other tribes of Kenya and Tanzania trace their origin. It is interesting to note the way they preserve traditions, as well as the similarity between their rituals and those described in the Old Testament.

For Africans, song, dance, and rhythm are indispensable to a Eucharistic celebration. The people writhed with emotion upon hearing in their own language the story of the passion, death and resurrection of Jesus Christ and upon discovering details of his life so similar to their own pastoral history. On Holy Thursday, the Last Supper and the Washing of the Feet were performed in African style. Members of each generation of the populace were made to sit on blocks of stone and upon a goat skin we placed a milk-filled pumpkin and a pot of *ugali*, a kind of corn meal batter. These symbols were more meaningful to them. Then, groups of women and members of the small neighboring communities came to adore Jesus, the Good Shepherd, at Mass.

The most interesting and moving moments influencing all that transpired during the Easter celebration were the effective integration of Old Testament tradition and the introduction of Christ into native cultural life. From early afternoon, all the members of the tribe had been congregating in the mission church area; it was the first time that warriors, elders, women, adolescents and children had gathered together in a celebration of this kind. According to tribal custom, warriors are prohibited from sharing nourishment with women, including their own mothers.

Each generation, and representatives from every basic community, prepared an activity to be mutually enjoyed, whether it is singing, dancing, or drama.

Following the Old Testament

At sunset, the elders of the tribe brought forth a sacrificial lamb, in order to celebrate the *sorrio* (Feast of the Paschal Lamb), as is described in the Book of Exodus 12 :1-14.

A solid-colored male animal was offered as atonement for the people's sins; after its throat was slit, its blood was smeared on the poles representing church pillars, and on the upper half of the church door. Then we dabbed blood on the forehead and chest of the elders, a sign of their conversion, more meaningful to them than if we were to use ashes.

The elders start a fire, in the traditional primitive manner of rubbing two sticks together. This fire is identified as the new light of Jesus Christ and from it, we will light the Paschal Candle. The animal is then roasted and the entire community dines on the young goat, leaving nothing for the next day.

The use of these symbols facilitates the explanation of Jesus as the New Paschal Lamb who dies for our sins and whose resurrection unites us daily in prayer so that we may live a better life through the celebration of the Eucharist, and by following his Word. His blood is a sign of reconciliation, and union with Christ and our fellow man.

All this joy and cultural richness can only be felt through the excitement of living His life story at Easter time. Words cannot sufficiently express Jesus' repeated death and resurrection, especially in such cultures where mention of the Son of God has scarcely begun.

God's grace

Holy Week celebrations and the happiness that comes at the culmination of the Feast of the Resurrection provided this small nascent community with a unique occasion for growing in the faith. The colorful, abundant signs and symbols make it a rich experience that fills one's heart; a unique adventure for us, occurring just once-in-a lifetime, it can only be felt by traveling deep into the heart of the semi-desert. The satisfaction we feel and the spiritual rewards the poor give us, a consumer society could never purchase nor imagine to be possible.

If life in our country and other parts of the world becomes more difficult, my wish is that hope and happiness prevail. Things have been difficult here for a long time, but we are steadfast in our determination to make life a little better for everyone. May the Resurrected Jesus, Victor over Death, forever reside within us.

After experiencing Easter in this traditional culture, thanks to the Grace of God, I am elated to be able to share with you how our hope, faith and optimism regarding the future evangelization of these people, children of Nkai, has grown stronger.

Father Jorge Fernández with a group of new Christians from the Suyian settlement about 15 kilometers (9 1/2 mi.) from the center of Barsaloi, during the celebration of Holy Week.

EATING TOGETHER,
AN UNACCEPTABLE CUSTOM

Food is surely one of the most important signs of friendship, love and unity, and eating together is a prized tradition among many people. To eat in the company of others means accepting to share one's life, as well as fraternity and forgiveness. Nevertheless, there is an exception to every rule. Among the Samburu, it is unacceptable for men, women, adolescents and children to eat together. On this point, certain rules and taboos must be observed if punishment is to be avoided.

When a woman gives birth, the tribe celebrates the important, joyous occasion, but her husband must not remain in the house, or anywhere nearby. One of the women will advise him that his wife has brought a child into this world, and to show the people the child's sex, he must then draw blood from a cow if the newborn is female; in the case of a male, he must extract it from a bull. Later, the women will visit the new mother, taking her gifts. That same day, or shortly thereafter, the husband must sacrifice an animal, generally a lamb, to be eaten solely by the women.

A wedding ceremony is a community-wide celebration. The groom sacrifices a calf in front of the bride's home, signifying the union, but neither bride nor groom must partake of the meat. The children are given the heart to eat, and the best portions are reserved for the tribal elders. That evening, a ceremony will be held within the camp; around the fire the elders pray, chat and share the roasted meat. It is a traditional *watan*, where only the tribal elders of a certain age are present. Warriors and shepherd girls dance both before and after the ceremony, but are not invited to share the roasted lamb. The newly-wed groom is prohibited from taking nourishment in the presence of his bride until the taboo or *Lmenon*, is lifted. The celebration of this ritual can only be held once the couple goes to live in their *Nkaji naibor*, or "white house." They invite family and friends to celebrate, as the bride prepares meat or an appropriate special food, from which the groom offers a portion to his bride, and vice-versa, in the presence of the applauding guests. From now on, the bride and groom will be able to share meals together. The celebration of this privilege ceremony has been known to be delayed for several months.

For fifteen years Samburu males are classified as warriors, who must undergo various rituals signifying increased maturity during this stage of their lives. Called *Lmug'iet*, these ceremonies consist of a series of blessings and the sacrifice of one or more animals whose flesh is distributed by age groups, with each member of the family receiving a determined share. But the young men must partake of their meal in the woods, far from the view of the females.

In this culture, it is unacceptable for warriors to eat in the presence of married women, or for the women to approach the area where circumcised young men are sacrificing an animal or preparing a meal. Yet, these males can eat in the presence of, or share meals with, uncircumcised females who, in many cases, are their betrothed, though they are not yet eligible to be married.

Once circumcised, a fourteen or fifteen-year old male must not partake of any food in the presence of a married woman, including his own mother. According to many accounts, this incredibly strange custom has its origin in a period of extreme drought when food was very scarce and mothers secretly shared what little they had with their frailest children. The warriors were sent to fend for themselves in the forest, or to tend the herds in other areas.

Some say that this custom permits the polygamous elders to regulate contact between their young wives and the warriors. A warrior must never enter a married woman's home alone, and only then to drink tea or milk. A warrior will never eat sweets in the presence of children or other persons, who believe the formers' diet is limited to milk, blood and meat. The elderly who govern the tribe always include an animal sacrifice when arriving at a decision and consequently, they eat the best portions of the meat. Within the family unit, the roasted head of a sacrificed kid-goat or lamb becomes the husband's property, while the other members of the household share the rest of the animal.

There also exist other ceremonies and sacrifices in which each group of society plays a specific role and has its own area for taking meals. All of these customs and traditions are frequently in conflict with the evangelization process. ¿How is it possible to present and inculturate the Eucharist within the tribes' culture? It has been tried, and many have acquiesced as believers in the Word of God. "In the Eucharist, that is, in Christ, there is no slave or free man, Hebrew or Greek, man or woman (Galatians 3 :28)".

During the Last Supper ceremony of Holy Week, the apostles were played by men, women, warriors, girls and boys of the tribe. The sharing in common of *ugali*, or corn batter and milk became a natural and spontaneous act. In this way, they were able to understand that the Eucharist is a symbol of unity and love. Dining together can therefore be understood by the Samburu to be a worthy custom.

At the banquet table of life, there can be no marginal nor excluded individuals.

An African Supper, by Jesus Mafa

During the Last Supper ceremony of Holy Week, the apostles were played by men, women, warriors, boys and girls from the tribe. The sharing in common of ugali, corn meal batter, and milk, became a natural and spontaneous act. In this way, the local people were then able to understand that the Eucharist is a symbol of unity and love.

AMONG SHEPHERDS AND LIONS

At Christmas time, the manger is a fundamental symbol for Christians. We have all seen a variety of mangers, some elaborated in many ways; others simple, to reflect more spiritually God's preference for the lowly, his birth "among us," divested of pride and grandeur. Other mangers are indicative of a consumer society, distorting the true meaning of the Lord's Incarnation.

While celebrating Christmas with the Samburu, among shepherds and shepherdesses, the poor and marginalized, it is much easier to understand the Gospel stories telling of Jesus' birth more than twenty centuries ago. Bethlehem easily relates both in culture and religion to the reality we live here. In fact, geographically, it is also quite close to us.

According to the writings of Luke (2 :1-20), in regard to the birth of Christ, he tells us that there were in the area many shepherds who slept in the open fields and who "tended their flocks by night." This is a familiar story here, among the shepherds, sheep and lions.

The semi-nomadic shepherds move about constantly with their herds, in search of pasture and water. In their wanderings, nature is their habitat; the moon, sun and stars, their protection.

At night, they rest in *Lale,* or clearings surrounded by brier patches, seeking refuge for their herds from the lions, cheetahs and leopard

Saint Luke relates how the shepherds were the first to receive the announcement of the birth of Christ. "And it came to pass, when the angels had departed from them into heaven, that the shepherds were saying to one another, 'Let us go over to Bethlehem, and see this thing that has come to pass, which the Lord has made known to us.' So they went with haste and found Mary and Joseph, and the babe lying in the manger (Luke 2 :15-16)". The Samburu huts are similar to those of Bethlehem. The people build their *manyatas* with poles, branches, cow dung and earth. This becomes temporary housing for the shepherds and their newborn lambs.

When a Samburu mother gives birth, she places the child on a cow hide, commonly its bed, and wraps it in a sheepskin. As was true for the Son of God, these children are born in poverty and simplicity, marginal and forgotten. It is easy to see the humble God, the "Emmanuel" (Isaiah 7 :14) in the *manyatas* of the Samburu.

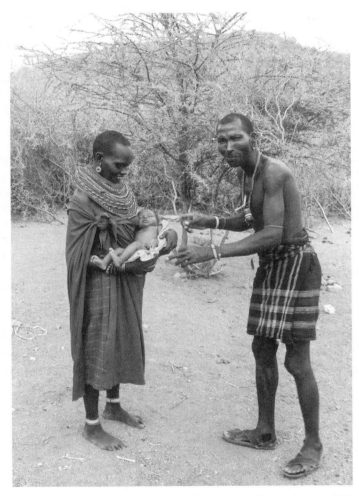

Samburu shepherds experience the joy of a new child.
Like the Son of God, these children are born into
simplicity and poverty, marginalization and obscurity.

BAPTIZING WITH WATER AND MILK

In mid-July, 1996, I celebrated fourteen youth and adult baptisms in a village called Suyian, a word meaning gray. It is known for a wild dog of the same name, perhaps deriving from the color of the animal's coat. In this extremely arid region, we met every week over a period of two years in order to offer religious instruction to those wishing to receive Baptism, Confirmation and Communion The inhabitants were overjoyed, and I witnessed the growth of this small community, formerly of only twenty Christians, all the while conducting the ceremony in their native language.

The small community presented the songs accompanied by dancing. The water, somewhat yellowish as a result of drought conditions, was brought by one of the female catechumens from the river near Suyian. During the ceremony, I blessed the water, and then, according to custom, the natives brought forth a small amount of milk to be mixed with it. A water and milk baptism! The *nkarrer*, or water mixed with milk, has great significance for the Samburu, as all blessings are performed with that mixture. Water alone is important, but mixed with milk, it takes on a deeper meaning. The natives understand and accept this practice naturally. The new Christians became overjoyed, eager to become followers of Jesus Christ in the midst of their countrymen.

After two years in Kenya, I can understand the local language much better and have been able to pinpoint the essence of missionary life, something that one can discern during the preparatory years, but which reveals itself only in actual practice.

WHEN THE DESERT IS IN BLOOM

The blessing of Nkai's saliva has been pouring forth in abundance. For three weeks in June and July, it has rained tempestuously. The desert has begun to blossom, as recounted in the book of Isaiah, and the people are quite happy. Warriors dance with their shepherdesses during the day and all the families gather along with their herds in the evening. There is an abundance of milk and many family members return from afar, where they had gone in search of pasture land.

Nkai has showered us with rain, and the time is perfect for performing circumcisions, marriages, and blessings of the elders, under the moonlit and starry skies.

Unfortunately, amid so much happiness, the loss of life has been felt, in imitation of the Gospel story of the good shepherd giving his life to save that of his sheep. While trying to rescue their cattle, several young shepherds were dragged to their deaths by the turbulent waters. No one bothers to search for the cadavers, which will become fodder for the night-time beasts, if the sand does not bury them first.

The down-side of this season of the year is that the flooded roads make travel by motorcycle and automobile an impossibility. Taking care of a community's needs, and transporting the infirm to the hospital, become herculean tasks. It is often necessary to wait several hours for the waters to recede, or to repair large sections of the roadway with sand and stones. The quagmire is almost enough to force one to his knees and beseech God for the use of a helicopter. But for now, we must persevere and in dire cases, avail ourselves of a camel.

THE SEMI-DESERT TOMATOES

And Jesus said, "Thus is the Kingdom of God, as though a man should cast seed into the earth, then sleep and rise, night and day, and the seed should sprout and grow without his knowing it." (Mark 4 :26-27)

Farming in the semi-desert is quite difficult due to the lack of water and certain characteristics of the land, the greater part of which consists of stones and sand. More than ninety-five percent of the trees and plants possess thorns, prickly pears or tangled branches, causing danger everywhere. Even so, the land produces nourishment for all the animals: the herds and graceful gazelles, rabbits and deer, cattle and the feared buffalo, camels and giraffes, birds and ostriches, and even for the impressive elephants. The God who cares for all of his creatures, also makes it possible for men and women to live in the semi-desert. But planting and harvesting some crops in the semi-desert is a formidable task requiring patience, strength and faith.

In the mission garden we have succeeded in growing the most delicious fruit, based on ingenuity and hard work, and have shown the people by example, that it is possible, though not easy, to grow things. We recycle all our food waste, as well as household water, for all our waste water is used to irrigate the garden.

The massive rainstorms at the end of 1997 and the beginning of 1998, caused by the climatic phenomenon known as *El Niño*, caused the semi-desert to bloom as never before, and for the first time in decades, people were able to harvest corn, beans and sorghum, thanks to a favorable seed distribution plan and the invitation we at the mission made to the local people to plant crops.

Then something happened without our knowledge, and soon the area surrounding the mission and even far away regions were sprouting tomato plants whose fruit the local people gathered with great joy, thanks to the birds and other small animals.

To this day, I can vividly recall the time a Samburu woman from the district of Nairimirimo, about twenty-one kilometers (13 mi.) from our Barsaloi center, approached us, in order to show how many tomatoes she had gathered, saying to me, "Father, look at how far the Barsaloi tomatoes have spread, thanks to the birds who brought them from the mission garden to this place."

98

I was very moved by the experience and later, at evening prayer, I shared this fact of life and sign of God with my companions.

It is not part of their culture for semi-nomadic shepherds to farm. The earth produces trees and some pasture, but for a Samburu, cultivating the land means having to injure it. But little by little, the shepherds' feelings have begun to change, as they make contact with other tribes and experience other agricultural products such as corn and beans as part of their diet.

Evangelization is a slow process at times, requiring stamina, faith, methodology and patience on the part of the evangelizer. But the silent and mysterious work is carried out by the Holy Spirit, without our realizing it.

All of us are called upon to plant the seeds of justice, peace, solidarity, goodness, respect for life, and trust in God, if we wish for a changed world and a better future.

A NEW VEHICLE

Finally, after a long wait and constant problems with our old automobile, we have been able to acquire a new Toyota for our mission, thanks to the efforts of many benefactors. We limit the use of our vehicle to ambulance calls, long pastoral trips or when the need arises, to stock up on medicine, fuel and other items needed at the mission.

Therefore, due to a limited budget, and in order to save on fuel and car maintenance costs, we continue to make regular visits to the villages by motorcycle.

Night on the Seya River

After the first thousand kilometers (about 625 mi.), it was time to give our new car its initial check-up. I left Barsaloi, headed for Nanyuki, a town of frigid climate and fertile land, near Mount Kenya. On the way back, I stopped at the Wamba hospital to pick up a young boy, Charles Ekwam, who was being discharged after having recuperated from a bout of tuberculosis. We arrived at the Seya River around four in the afternoon. It had rained in the mountains and the river's sand was moist. I put the car in four-wheel drive and gathered up speed in order to cross the two hundred meters (about 600 ft.) of sand. At about 30 meters (90 ft.) from where I began the crossing, the car stalled and three of the wheels sank into the sand. The tachometer read 1,514 kilometers. It was impossible to move at that moment. The makeshift winch was too short and could not reach as far as the opposite side of the river. I decided to remove all cargo from the car in order to lighten the load. Ekwam, still weak, could be of no help to me. Night arrived and the mosquitoes began to invade the region. The wild beasts began to produce numerous sounds, signifying it was dangerous to be outside. We settled as best we could inside the car, but noticed that river water was flowing beneath us. We were unable to sleep, for even inside the vehicle our lives were in danger. It was a long night. The next morning, Ekwam went to ask the elders of the place called Suari, to help us. They brought hot tea, and asked for almost one hundred dollars to help us get out. We had a long, heated discussion and I reminded them that I was not a tourist, but was working with the Samburu. Moreover, the boy I was taking home from the hospital was not paying a cent. Finally, I gave them the little money I had on me, about thirty dollars. By afternoon, I was able to get to the mission. Even with a new vehicle, one can suffer in the semi-desert. At times, the mission is full of surprises. One never knows what will happen.

This calling to introduce the Gospel to the Dark Continent, is a gift and a commitment at the same time. I have felt a wonderful interior rejuvenation, a happiness that I have felt very few times in my life, a more profound and encompassing experience of God.

AN AURA OF VIOLENCE

During the stage of their lives as warriors, Samburu males fulfill a kind of military service. But even into adulthood they remain armed with spears, swords and knives in order to survive in the wooded areas where savage animals abound.

When encountering the armed men along the roadway, one should not fear the sight of them proudly carrying their traditional weapons. Their word of greeting will always be *serian*, meaning "peace." Unfortunately, for some time now, politicians have begun to supply the natives with firearms, mainly to help them protect their herds. It is common for these weapons to be utilized indiscriminately, resulting in trouble arising among neighbors who have lived side by side in peace, for years. Tranquility is disturbed, as arms manufacturers become richer.

Alarming tribal confrontation

In the first few months of 1996, many things have happened so quickly that one is left with the impression that a dam has burst or that the rapid thaw has provoked an avalanche capable of carrying away everything in its path. After many years of relative peace in the semi-desert, it now seems that destruction is everywhere, and that violence and tribal encounters, in extreme cases, can even cause us Missionaries of Yarumal, working at primary evangelization, to flee the area.

What has happened?
Sometime around the month of May there was a confrontation at Isiolo, in which several Samburu and Somalies were murdered, in addition to the theft of cattle carried out by the Somalies, causing the Samburu to emigrate to another region. In reprisal, the Samburu twice attacked the Somalies of Suyian, causing them to flee from this village which was part of our Barsaloi mission, and threatening those Somalies of Barsaloi with war, if they did not leave. The end result was that all Somalies were forced to leave both Barsaloi and Suyian.

According to highly trustworthy sources, the Samburu attacked and left wounded a large number of Somalies on the outskirts of the village of Lodongokwe. Some reports stated that there were deaths on both sides, but it has been proven that the Samburu stole more than three thousand head of cattle.

Since August, many people were slain and cattle theft has not subsided. Fearful of being attacked and stripped of their only wealth, large groups have emigrated to other regions. From our mission, the inhabitants of six villages abandoned their campsites or *manyatas*. While the Samburu were stealing and attacking on one front, the Turkana arrived and made off with thousands of cattle belonging to Samburu and Rendille natives in the vicinity of Baragoi and the Valley of Tears, which at the time was incredibly green.

The Turkana have continued the offensive near Tuum, Baragoi and in the vicinity of Barsaloi. In addition, the Samburu have begun to utilize their arms to steal cattle from other Samburu and to fire weapons during the night. The government has sent police squads to Marti and Baragoi, and an army detachment to Tuum and South Horr. But the attacks and cattle rustling have continued. In the vicinity of Marti, several Samburu were wounded and a little girl was killed. Near Suyian, on October 1, the day following the Marti attack, the Turkana came, murdering a married woman and a young boy, and stealing all the cattle belonging to the *manyatas* there.

There is no longer a soul living in the area of Simiti. Suyian has reverted to a ghost town whose chapel is a silent witness to what the place could have become, but did not.

In summary, the people have been forced to move elsewhere and according to the elders, the situation continues to be extremely tense, as ever more commonly, the people of Barsaloi must emigrate as well.

Live combat

While I am writing, the tribal elders have interrupted me to relay the latest developments: The Samburu have gone to the Marti mountains to confront the Turkana, resulting in the deaths of five Turkana and four Samburu. The latter have carried off more that three hundred head of cattle belonging to their rivals. The situation is serious; even as we attempt to remain calm by relying on the Lord, we realize that we might have to emigrate as well, and would also be in danger.

It is now necessary to avoid traveling at night, even to transport the infirm. As the violence increases around us, we find it hard to believe how our people are selling their animals in order to buy rifles. In the face of such difficult situations, there is always a ray of hope. And for this reason, we missionaries prefer to stay put and continue to accompany our people.

LEAVE, FOR THEY ARE
GOING TO KILL YOU

On December 3, 1996, a huge massacre took place in a village located about eighty kilometers (50 mi.) from Barsaloi. After having suffered several attacks and the theft of their cattle by the neighboring Turkana tribe, the Samburu took up arms, and supported by members of the Pokot and Rendille tribes, attempted to avenge themselves against the Turkana. According to newspaper reports fifty-eight people were slaughtered in that massacre, the majority of whom were women and children. Other sources maintain that one hundred seventy-eight people were murdered that day, though more believable is a report made by other individuals who went to the area of the massacre and took photos of the victims. Their evidence raised the number killed to approximately two hundred forty. On the night of December third, several Samburu who had participated in the massacre came to Barsaloi and began to incite the people. "The Turkana are following us and are coming to kill you," they said. "What has happened there is quite terrible. Many people have been slaughtered and the Tarkana are seeking vengeance. It would be better if you left the area." At that point, the panic-stricken people began to arrive at the mission, asking for a place of refuge inside the church.

Our friends and employees were adamant in their warning to us. "Fathers, go, for they are going to kill you. Leave this place, now." After the initial shock and the voices of warning, we decided to meet on the mission terrace. "What do we do? Where shall we go?" we asked ourselves. Juan Carlos and Jairo suggested to me that we leave for somewhere. In the midst of such fright, though with great faith and a strong conviction that we could not abandon the people, I said to my companions, "I will not leave this place for anywhere else, and much less at night. I want to go to bed. God is not dead, nor is he ill. He will watch over all of us."

It was a long night. Then, on December 4, all the village residents left; only the missionaries and about six elders remained. From the mission center, we worked together to transport the elders and children to a nearby area, utilizing our car. Then we continued making visits to the people where they had relocated and attempted to provide the shepherds with company during such times of tension. This situation was unleashing a cycle of violence and vengeance, in which the poor and helpless suffer the most.

These were tense moments at the mission. From the nearly twenty villages in existence in 1996, only three remained. The majority of the people left for other areas of the semi-desert or the lofty mountains, where wild animals are abundant. They tell of a mother who entered the forest, after having walked for more than twelve hours. Exhausted from the trek, she fell asleep. During the night, an elephant killed this woman; one of its enormous feet trampled her to death.

We are not able to celebrate Christmas here as we would like to, and as is customary. We were awaiting the Prince of Peace, and got instead, the Satan of violence. Precisely in the early morning hours of December 25, more than six hundred armed men and boys attacked the Barsaloi region, killing various individuals. Some have reported fifteen people killed and twelve wounded, with more than twenty thousand animals carried off. Even the Yarumal Missionaries present in the Barsaloi region at the time were forced to flee to a nearby wooded area, alongside the housing of area residents, and in the midst of bullets and panic. Afterward, our job was to seek help and to take the wounded to the hospital at Wamba in our automobile/ambulance. Even though our task in a time of despair and panic was to attempt to offer a measure of hope and calm, one thing remains very clear: the people know their area well, and were positive their enemies would return.

On December 26, a helicopter was shot down, in which James Nyandoro, District Commissioner and mayor of the Samburu District, was traveling along with two other occupants, both members of the army. In response to the assault carried out by members of the Turkana tribe, the government sent hundreds of soldiers, armored tanks, planes and helicopters to the Sugata Valley region to fight against the attackers. According to the inhabitants of the Suguta Valley, the majority of the Turkana were slain, and almost all their cattle incinerated by the bombs launched by the army.

Hopeful signs

From the point of view of pastoral work, we should state that many of the efforts made in the various communities suffered a great setback, in human terms. Nevertheless, the inhabitants of the semi-desert remained grateful to us, and at a major gathering of the elders, stated: "Everyone abandoned us, the government, political leaders, and private agencies. Only the missionaries stayed here with us. We thank you very much for living among us."

In moments of suffering and tension, the natives have approached the mission with trust, requesting help or merely asking permission to seek refuge in the churches and small chapels.

Thanks to God, through our efforts, many of the wounded, especially the young, were saved and little by little are returning to their work as students or keepers of their herds.

They are smiling again. Our relation to the people has changed, also. They perceive us as closer, and our friendship has grown. We are greater friends. With God's help we shall continue to sow the seeds of the Good News, even though the fruit of this labor seems scarce at times in this place of Primary Evangelization.

It is obvious that the situation in which the poor and the marginalized of the semi-desert find themselves, is not severe in comparison to what many refugees and displaced persons must face, not only in the countries surrounding the great African lakes, but also in our beloved Colombia and neighboring countries.

In spite of all the difficulties, the desire to live continues unabated. In this semi-desert, God's presence is so basic and apparent that we rejoice at times to the fact that we lack the comforts and conveniences that make slaves of modern society.

These local people have not lost their sense of humor, nor their engaging smiles. The warriors continue with their songs and dances, alongside their shepherdesses. Our garden, after months of constant care and irrigation, provides us with some of the most delicious fruit, to the envy of the most discerning palates: papayas, tangerines, oranges and an occasional watermelon are part of our diet. And if that weren't enough, mother nature regales us each morning with a concert provided by the most beautiful birds in the semi-desert. The fauna at times provide us with live, non-stop spectacles that are the envy of the most patient camera buffs. The *Ilakir le Nkai*, stars, or eyes of God, as the Samburu poetically refer to them, invite us to dream, converse, sing or continue dreaming, nightly. Can there possibly be a more beautiful transparent, starry sky than the one we view in the equatorial zone of the desert? The sky is the limit, for all who dream and believe.

REFUGEES IN THEIR OWN LAND

T ribal confrontation that year left many dead, and displaced thousands. These clashes increased both in intensity and viciousness, taking on the characteristics of open warfare, waged mainly by the Turkana, Samburu, Pokot, Rendille and Somali tribes, along with militarized troops of the Kenyan army.

All of the encounters, the slaughtering of people, cattle thievery and tribal displacement occurred principally in areas of the Samburu and Turkana districts of Northwestern Kenya. According to some reports, the fighting degenerated into guerrilla warfare, eventually becoming a threat to the government. The proliferation of illegal weapons in Kenya and all of Eastern Africa is a time bomb.

Bishop Ambrose Ravasi of the Diocese of Marsabit, where the warfare is continuing, says: "I have had the opportunity to visit many of the affected areas. I have felt the necessity to go there immediately after the most recent attack, fully aware of the unsettling situation in which the people find themselves. I hope that my presence will at least be a sign of trust and relief in the midst of their suffering, and that someone is thinking of them and cares for them. I am sincere when I say that I have never in my life seen people so frightened, confused and suspicious of one another."

It has always been rumored that cattle theft is endemic in those areas. In some ways, the practice has always been a part of the culture of the majority of the pastoral tribes. Nevertheless, a new twist has been added to what was once considered an innocent game. These new tactics, bordering on organized crime, consist of the use of sophisticated weapons, the destruction of homes and animals, the slaughter of women and children, sadistic deeds, and unprecedented organization and support. Some observers feel that the traditional practice of stealing one another's cattle now involves hate and ethnic cleansing instigated by political interests, ambition and corruption and resulting in a wide path of destruction, terror, the spilling of blood, and the resultant creation of thousands of displaced persons who have become refugees in their own land.

While in the Samburu district, I have had the opportunity to speak with many people, among them, civil and religious leaders, women, teachers, police, and the young, and all agree that these tribal clashes seem to be purposely well-planned, that personal safety is almost non-existent, and that the government, full of promises and lacking strength, seems helpless. Some individuals claim to know the identity of who is behind all this. Yet, it is difficult to ascertain the truth. Nevertheless, many people from all walks of life have asked me to speak out on their behalf, fearful of persecution, if they were to do it openly themselves.

Illnesses such as malaria, tuberculosis, diarrhea, typhoid and AIDS, are increasing as a result of the lack of potable water and the deplorable conditions surrounding the refugees of the semi-desert. The work of missionaries and pastoral care agencies is minimal in the face of the magnitude of the problems. Some individuals have sought refuge in the churches.

For many of the displaced, faced with constant central government neglect, the tribal strife will continue to be instigated by political leaders.

Lowly huts in a Turkana settlement near the lake of the same name.
This region of Northern Kenya, famous for its paleontological
discoveries, is referred to as the cradle of humankind.

TEN CHILDREN AND THEIR CATTLE

The first rains will soon be coming, after several months of drought. Multiple clouds now cover this area of the semi-desert, and people and animals are preparing for the task of returning to their former homes, where water and pasture will then reappear.

The relative calm that has been in effect for quite some time now in our region, has recently been interrupted by an attack on one of our villages. Initially, a warrior was slain and several hundred animals taken. The day after the attack, the tribal elders approached us asking for assistance, as ten young shepherds were missing. With God's help we searched and found them, hungry, tired from their nighttime travel and trying to collect the few animals the perpetrators were unsuccessful in stealing. One of the shepherds had been miraculously saved. A bullet that pierced his clothing was stopped by a small knife the child was carrying with him.

Our missionary presence has often presented us with similar situations capable of changing our plans from one moment to the next, but we always try to be with the people, especially in times of suffering. What is going to transpire from now on? Perhaps fear will return to many communities. Nevertheless, we hope the present situation will soon change for the better. The people of Barsaloi will almost certainly never emigrate, and we shall try our best to continue with our labors with dedication and faith. Unfortunately, the problems of the present time are not new to the area, and little by little, we are learning to work around the difficulties.

TRIBALISM, AN AFRICAN EVIL

The shepherds teach us to live, and to be less concerned with the concept of time. What has not been easy for these simple people is the constant presence of difficulties in their lives, though they don't seem to be giving up, or becoming bitter.

In various places throughout Kenya, the drought has been continuing and the people are worried that they and the animals will suffer greatly from the lack of food and water. In normal times, the drought lasts until the month of April in our area, which means that at this time of the year everything is dry and the temperature, especially during the day, always rises above thirty degrees centigrade (86 degrees F). Nighttime temperatures are conducive to sleep, with temperatures hovering around twenty degrees centigrade. (68 F).

To our dismay, clashes between the neighboring Samburu and Turkana tribes have been intensifying and the people are again living nightmares. The rustling of cattle is almost always accompanied by shooting, and at times, the wounding and killing of adversaries. In our residential area of Barsaloi, the people refuse to venture out and all their cattle are kept in special places. During the last attack about seven kilometers (4 mi.) from Barsaloi, three people were left wounded and nearly one thousand animals stolen. It was up to us to coordinate the task of transporting the wounded to the hospital. Although some of the animals were recovered, the inhabitants of other villages have gone to the mountains and the forested regions where they are competing for space with savage beasts. A few days ago, two people were killed by buffalo, which are as feared here as the lion is.

It is obvious that the attacks and mutual distrust are the fault of both sides. On December 30, 1999, for example, large numbers of Samburu, estimated at some three hundred, attacked Kawap, a Turkana camp ministered by our colleagues from the Tuum mission. Although the Samburu succeeded in stealing a large number of animals, they were surprised by the Turkana and the Kenyan army, resulting in more than twenty of them killed, some from our villages.

Such attacks were a part of life in these villages where cattle theft was considered an act of bravery, and acceptable when carried out against one's enemies. At times, such thievery was carried out within the tribe itself, where it is punished and the perpetrator or perpetrators must pay a fine of many animals. The big problem lies in the fact that the chosen weapon for this type of war has changed. Until a few years ago, everything was accomplished with the spear and bow and arrow, resulting in fewer deaths. At the present time, arms manufacturers have established a profitable business, and shepherds have found it necessary to acquire modern arms for self-defense and to protect their animals. Some time ago, Pope Paul VI proclaimed a prophetic warning: " If humanity does not put an end to war, war will put an end to humanity." Nothing seems to change the hearts of exporters and promoters of the business of war. In addition, the televised version of war is now regarded as a spectacle, to be enjoyed impassively in the comfort of one's home.

Why must the poorest and most marginal suffer so much? And while all of this is happening, economic neo-liberalism speaks to us of silent majorities, unproductive people, non-functional tribes and people without a future.

How does this speak to our faith? Much or little, depending upon personal or community commitment. In the view of pessimists, everything is lost, because economic competition, distorted by inequality, gives no hope for living to the poorest of the poor. Others of us believe that we have been called upon to be purveyors of good, to value people for what they are, to recognize cultural diversity as wealth, to bravely confront the problems arising from violence and to explore their causes, to become humble instruments in discovering and expressing God's tenderness, all the while united as an influential force. As men and women of the missions, we are committed to Jesus' ideal world. We believe in the universal brotherhood and sisterhood of mankind, and adopt fathers, mothers, brothers and sisters to take the place of our own family. Love belies the myth of "out of sight, out of mind."

We wish to continue our task in this region of Primary Evangelization. Though life itself is hazardous, we feel at peace, confident in being the bridge to unite these tribes formerly living in harmony for years, now seeing themselves manipulated by leaders in pursuit of self-interest. In the two missions of Barsaloi and Tuum, we Missionaries of Yarumal minister to members of both the Samburu and Turkana tribes. In Tuum, for example, there are two housing complexes, Kawap and Parkati, belonging to the Turkana. At present, we missionaries are the only people who can circulate from one tribe to the other without causing suspicion and mistrust.

In the month of January, I took the chance of saying Mass for the first time in the Turkana language and preaching in Samburu. Mass formerly was said in Swahili, the national language of Kenya, but was understood by only a few. Our pastoral challenge here is great, learning Turkana and introducing Jesus in the language of the people even though their housing areas in our missions are sparse. While many of the Turkana understand the Samburu language, the opposite is not true. The Turkana are stronger and more numerous, less refined in features, yet capable of adapting to different situations.

For years now, they have been gaining ground on the Samburu; that is, moving from the desert to the semi-desert. Tribal wealth, unfortunately, has come to the point of tribalism, the source of many of Africa's problems. European colonizers are greatly responsible for this tribal upheaval. "Blood is thicker than water."

We missionaries believe in the universal brotherhood of man, and adopt numerous others as fathers, mothers, brothers and sisters to take the place of our family. Love belies the myth of "out of sight, out of mind."

I LEAVE MY BODY TO THE HYENAS

One morning after prayer, a woman arrived at the mission residence, carrying her four-year old son in her arms. She stated her son was very ill and needed to see the male-nurse at once. I showed her how to get to the health center and in a few minutes the nurse arrived with the boy's letter of admission to the Wamba hospital, some eighty-five kilometers (51mi.) away.

The diagnosis was meningitis. In addition, the child's condition had deteriorated as a result of the natives' belief that when a child is ill - especially a boy - it is a good idea to remove the tonsils, a procedure performed without anesthesia and under unsanitary conditions.

Once the car was ready, I left for the hospital with the mother and her dying child. It always seems that the more urgent it is to save a life, the longer and more treacherous the sandy, rocky roads become. And the sun was hotter than ever. We had traveled some fifty kilometers (30 mi.) when the child went into a coma. A bit farther, the woman said to me, "*Intasho! Ketepero nkerai ai.*" "Stop, please, my child has died!"

My surprise increased when she asked me to open the car door. She got out and carried the cadaver into the nearby woods. Overcome with grief, she placed her son beneath a tree and returned immediately. As it customary in this tribe, they never transport a cadaver from one place to another; that night the hyenas would eat well.

And that ancestral custom is still practiced today. Ordinarily, when someone dies, they wrap the body in an animal skin and leave it in the grassland or the woods. Only in special cases is an elder buried in the camp where he lived. Nevertheless, an adult male, with numerous children and cattle, known as a *Lkimaita*, will be remembered by the tribe.

A female with children, known as an *Ntang' atana*, will also be buried. But even in this case, the woman will be discriminated against and no one will remember her, for as in the Old Testament, she will be comparable to a child. The worst thing that can happen to a Samburu - and this is true of other African tribes a well - is to die without leaving any descendants.

A young girl who dies is known as an *Ndorrop sesen*, or "small body." A deceased warrior is referred to as a laing' oni, signifying calf, and young children who die are referred to as *Lmuwarani*. It is prohibited to call a dead person by name. The Samburu never refer to a dead person as having died. And in normal conversation the dead are never referred to, nor named, and all of their belongings are disposed of. Death is final for them. Yet, they employ two distinct verbs for a person's death and that of an animal. *Ketepero Itungani*, means the person went to sleep. *Ketua Iowaru*, an animal disappeared.

The majority of African tribes believe in communicating with their ancestors. The deceased continue to be part of the community; that is, immortality and life after death are accepted. The intercession of ancestors is invoked at the most transcendental moments of a person or of the community.

As a result of the death of Father Carlos Alberto Calderón, who shared, loved and lived his last year with the members of this traditional tribe, the Samburu began to see death in a different light. At times they would express their feelings with the words, *Ketepero tenebo Nkai* or, he went to sleep in God, together with God. And also, *Keti ninye tenebo Nkai o tenebo iyioo*, meaning, He is with God and with us.

Others also said to us, "*Kayieu naaipot nkerai ai Carlos*," which means I want to give my son the name Carlos. And even though we appreciate from a cultural standpoint the names from the vernacular, we did not object to people wishing to call their sons Carlos.

In light of the African Synod, and the efforts being made to inculturate the faith, Bishop Bonifacio Haushiku, of Namibia, stresses: "African Christians must be permitted to freely and openly venerate their ancestors as part of Christian life, so that they may become truly Christian and remain authentically African." Here in Africa I have learned to value life as the most beautiful gift of God and to understand death as that "sister," not to be feared in excess.

In the process of Primary Evangelization, the moment is arriving in which to present Jesus as the elder, the ancestor, the conqueror of death, he who lives and is part of the community and who can be invoked at all times.

GOD'S TIME

During its period as a British colony, the small settlement of Barsaloi, with barely twelve hundred inhabitants, was the capital of the Samburu district. Its advantageous position in the heart of the region was the principal reason why the British chose it as the seat of the district government. Later, due to problems with the local people, malaria, and the arrival of merchants at Maralal, the district capital was transferred there.

In 1973, the first Catholic missionary settled in the area and began a program of evangelization and development. Schools, as well as two dispensaries, were built and some centers of religious instruction were established, along with their respective chapels. For many years the British had prohibited the entry of missionaries into the area. The natives were left to chance, on the reservations. But schooling and development were offered to the fertile-zone tribes or to the members of the same tribes as Presidents Kenyatta and Moi, during almost forty years of independence.

The semi-nomadic and pastoral tribes experienced very different living conditions from those of the sedentary and agricultural tribes in the center of the country, and in some ways a stagnation in education, health and development. The Samburu are among the most traditional and marginal of the tribes, and the few leaders among them are known to manipulate, deceive and exploit them. Some Samburu have had the opportunity to study, and occupy governmental posts, but it is very common to see members of President Moi's party, the Kalenjin, occupying the most influential positions throughout the country. Moi, in reality, is a dictator who has occupied the presidency since 1978. His decision to step down after 24 years as president of Kenya is seen across Africa as a moment of hope, a sign that the country can turn back toward democracy. At the end of 2002, Mwai Kibaki, 71, was elected as the new president of Kenya. Mr. Kibaki belongs to the Kikuyu, Kenya's main tribe, and won the presidency under the opposition movement, the National Rainbow Coalition.

Injustice, corruption and manipulation are forever present in the Primary Evangelization process among the poor and marginal. Time passes endlessly bringing no relief from suffering and injustice, and people feign a kind of resignation that can exasperate the evangelizing missionary convinced of the Kingdom of God's message. "When will these people wake up and keep the

114

leaders and merchants from exploiting and manipulating them?" the pastoral workers ask themselves. But human's time is not God's time, and for this reason one's work must be constant, arduous, and intelligent, trusting always in the actions of the Holy Spirit.

In turn, every culture presents the occasion for sin, traditions contrary to life, and institutionalized disregard for basic human rights. The missionary, as the evangelization advocate, is a presenter, a promoter of life, and therefore must work closely with both leaders and community, so that the latter might become an agents for change and freedom. At the beginning, the steps may seem very simple, rudimentary and slow, but the important thing is to respect the people's actions.

The natives of Barsaloi remember how a few years ago the bosses and owners of businesses were all members of the Somali tribe of Kenya, who in their unique position, exploited and abused the Samburu. The Yarumal Missionaries, during one of their formative lessons, asked the Samburu why they did not open a business in their own area and thus serve their people by reducing the high cost of food. They replied, "We do not know how, and we have always been shepherds, not businessmen." After taking some time to prepare, they opened several community stores and even in the mission, opened a small store. Tension grew high with the Somalis, and many of their Samburu friends, upon seeing the former lose customers denounced the missionaries and tried to discredit them with all sorts of accusations. The local people, now able to procure food more cheaply, united in their accusations against the tribal elders they considered to be friends of the exploiters. Some Samburu have now learned how to conduct business. Today, they have become the ones who buy and sell. The mission store was temporary, now no longer in existence. The Somalis have emigrated to another region where they own the businesses.

In regard to governmental aid, the region's political leaders are the ones who have controlled and taken advantage of the populace. For many years, they have stolen from the people a huge portion of the food sent by the government and international agencies. People are afraid to speak out, and if they criticize something, the politicians punish them by denying them the meager portion of corn or beans they are entitled to during times of drought.

Since all official bureaus, and businesses dealing in animals and food products, are concentrated in Maralal, the Samburu district's capital, the region's leaders spend the greater part of the year in that city, and have almost completely forgotten the rest of their people. We missionaries are the only outsiders who support the people. We have come to share the Good News of Jesus, and not to act as tourists.

When something happens, the people come to the mission, whether it be to share their happiness, or to shed tears during times of sadness.

Tribal tensions began seriously in 1996. It seems that the politicians are charged with inciting these tribal confrontations in order to further their own interests. For many years, the tribal members lived in peace. There were many mixed marriages, and a great respect for each tribe's traditions. At times, the tension caused by the threat of an attack reaches dramatic heights, and the people feel unprotected, as much by the impotent, ineffective, central government as by the leaders who do not live among the people, and who think only of their own welfare. All of this accumulated suffering has made many tribal members clamor for their rights and ask why there is so much injustice. The Kenyan Episcopal Conference has been developing a public awareness program for several years, focusing on justice, human rights, and building peace. This process has borne fruit, and in many places the condemnation of corruption and the democratization process have become firmly rooted.

In Barsaloi, people have joined together to demand their rights and a governmental presence. But civil leaders have chosen to consider priests and mission directors as instigators of this process, and consequently have banded together to discredit and slander the work of the Catholic Church, even going as far as to offer certain individuals money and food.

Ravages of the drought

During the year 2000, Kenya experienced the worst drought ever recorded, and many areas suffered a period of hunger brought about by this phenomenon. The government has asked international agencies, in particular, the United Nations, for help. One of the conditions for providing assistance is that government employees should not be involved in the food distribution, thereby lessening the chances of corruption. Instead, non-governmental agencies and the Church were charged with distributing and monitoring the humanitarian aid, along with the help of local committees comprised especially of women. This system had excellent results, and generally speaking, the poor and marginal received their entitlement of food during this severe famine.

Nevertheless, local government leaders tried through various means to regain control of the food distribution in order to cheat and manipulate the masses. Some of them even banded together to create an unfavorable environment for those in charge of the food allocations.

Throughout the month of August, Father Jorge Fernández had been mentioned in national news broadcasts as being responsible for the people of Barsaloi and other areas, not receiving their allotments of food. The regional councilor had paid a district news reporter to spread this information. This action was definitely meant to turn the people against the mission and to seek revenge for the outcry against corruption that had been heard in the community at that time.

In the face of such slander, the people united in their efforts not to accept the involvement of governmental leaders in food distribution. At the request of Fr. Jorge, United Nations representatives and the director of the Samburu district program came to the area for the purpose of verifying the truth, and also to listen to the community. The natives unanimously supported the presence and coordinating efforts of the Catholic Church and declared their pleasure at having received their fair share of food, without suspicion of corruption, for the first time in years.

Several weeks later, the local leaders came to the area to offer explanations and solicit the peoples' support. To their great surprise many people, especially the women who have no voice nor vote at any of the meetings, rose to tell the leaders, "You are nothing but thieves and we don't want to have any part of you, nor of the dishonest deals that go on in Maralal, the district capital. We shall continue to follow Fr. Jorge and the missionaries, because they live among us and will not deceive us. Even if Fr. Jorge's direction were to cause us to fall into a precipice, we would follow after him and will accept no other mediation for the distribution of food, than that of the Catholic Church. You may depart from this place, for we want no cheap political shenanigans here, and much less, corruption at the cost of hunger and death for our children."

The governmental leaders were embarrassed, to say the least, and the only words they could utter were, "We have never seen anything like this. Where did these semi-desert shepherds get this kind of wisdom? This is incredible."

The people have banded together to celebrate their faith and to offer up to God - Nkai - all the suffering they have endured during this time of drought. The community rejoices in knowing that together they will continue to discover how liberation becomes a reality.

Part

"I feel that my decision to go to Africa is making me experience God's love and tenderness more intensely. I am leaving without any hero or martyr complex, but rather, with the desire to discover the seeds of the Word in African cultures."

"If all of us who wish to follow Jesus only were more human, more united in our support of the weak, simpler in our manner of being, stronger fighters for justice, more contemplative, more fraternal, less arrogant, less money-hungry and less ambitious for power."

"If the grain of wheat dies not....."

Let the seed die
and may the opportune
moment arrive;
the spring ear will return
ten grains for one.
See how sweet the wait becomes,
when the signs are certain;
keep your eyes peeled
and your heart consoled:
If Christ has risen,
so, too, will the dead arise.

Let life blossom
As the years glide by,
such mild disappointments,
are but a burning obscenity.
Behold the Flowering Easter,
Flooding gardens in color;
keep your eyes alert
and your heart awake:
If Christ has risen,
so, too, will the dead arise.

Let this friend go forth
in peace, to a new land;
he will be with you forever
though his body shall depart.
See how brief the test
and how swift the ruffle.
Keep arms wide open
and a peaceful heart.
If Christ has risen,
so, too, will the dead arise.

Let time, that
generous and restful friend,
transform your anguish into joy,
keeping its sorrow within.
Whoever has died is now witness
beneath vast open skies,
that all his wrongs
the Lord has remedied:
If Christ has risen,
so, too, will the dead arise.

Let faith's light guide you
through life's journey;
keep it always bright
in order to reach the summit.
Let vanish that rust
acquired in the deserts
of this tormented world:
If Christ has risen,
so, too, will the dead arise.

Let love perform the task,
unmoved by time and space,
of calming your deep anxiety
toward Him, who heals and recreates.
Let your longing discern
the spirits of the departed.
Keep your eyes peeled
toward the starry sky.
If Christ has risen,
so, too, will the dead arise.

(From the Liturgy of the Hours)

"I AM DYING COMPLETELY HAPPY"

I am writing these words to share the role of Easter of Our Lord Jesus Christ in the death and resurrection of our friend and brother, Carlos Alberto. From the time of his joyous arrival in Kenya, I had the pleasure of being his companion during his residency at the mission, in studying the Masai language, and also his illness. I was able to be with him throughout his stay at the Wamba hospital, before he fell into a coma, and also when he was transferred to Nairobi. I was witness to the vastness of his faith and of his deep humanity, all of which obliges me to make these memories come alive again.

In the middle of 1994, we received notification of the arrival in Kenya of Father Carlos Alberto, an associate priest from the Archdiocese of Medellín, Colombia, as a member of the team of Yarumal Missionaries working in this East African country. We were happy to hear the good news, and though most of us did not know him personally, we had heard of his commitment to serving the poor and marginalized, and of his difficulties a few years previously, with Cardinal López Trujillo, as well as his efforts to lead a life of complete dedication to Jesus Christ.

In September of that year he said goodbye to his many Colombian friends, and stopped off in London for two months to brush up on his English. He arrived in Kenya on November 2, happy, optimistic, and uncomplicated as he was. We Yarumal Missionaries welcomed him as a member of our team and rejoiced in his decision to work with us on the "dark continent." He spent a month visiting Longisa and Abosi, our two missions serving the Kipsigis tribe, and where two other priests from the Archdiocese of Medellín, David Estrada and Orlando Morales, were assigned. Initially, Carlos Alberto was to work in Abosi.

In mid-December, we all left for Barsaloi, in Northwestern Kenya, in order to celebrate Christmas with the Samburu tribe. The encounter with the poverty, the semi-desert, the environment of Primary Evangelization, and above all, the people of this tribe convinced him his mission should be in Barsaloi. During the holiday period of Christmas and New Year's, he confided to me that he had reached a final decision after the death of "The Beautiful One," as his mother was affectionately called by his family. And from the very beginning of his experience in Barsaloi he had thought of remaining with the Samburu.

122

In Easter, 1995, Carlos Alberto was to write: "In my first letter to everyone, I told them I would be beginning my work among the Kipsigis tribe, at the Abosi mission in the southern part of the country and close to the Tanzanian border; I have changed my mind. At the beginning of the year, after attending a planning meeting and also because of an unexpected emergency at the Barsaloi mission, the team asked me to change my destination; I have accepted, and even though I had felt a slight attachment to the very friendly and warm Kipsigis, I am nevertheless happy to go to this new assignment. Along with the Masai, the Samburu constitute two of the most traditional tribes, not just of Kenya, but of the entire African continent. I am very happy to be at this "first encounter" mission, and to pursue the path to faith with these semi-nomadic communities."

Among the Masai

In mid-January, I went with Carlos to Lemek, in the heart of Masai country, to study the Maa language, which is very similar grammatically to that of the Samburu. He was extremely happy studying the language and knowing he was able to understand Masai culture a little better. At the mid-term break, we went to our Barsaloi mission to celebrate Holy Week and to practice Kisamburu. Carlos decided to spend time with the communities of Suyian and Simiti, two of the poorest and most arid villages in the desert.

When we returned to Lemek after the break, Carlos began to notice certain allergic reactions on his hands, lips and face. After the course of study was over, he submitted to a blood test aimed at identifying the cause of the inflammation, and all results proved negative. He decided he would have to live with the annoyance, although the rest of us thought it might have been an allergy to a certain condiment. Nevertheless, the problem continued, although without any noticeable damage to his health, nor lessening of his usual high spirits.

After our annual trip to Mombasa in the month of July, we returned to finish the Kimasai language course, and in August, we began to work at the Barsaloi mission, all the while continuing to study Kisamburu.

On the terrace of our living quarters the team united in prayer daily, and then shared the day's experiences. Carlos seemed to become increasingly happy and fulfilled in following the way of Jesus among the beautiful Samburu people. He had truly become one of the team. It wasn't unusual to see him cook on our trips to the house in Nairobi, or on our day off, at the house of our female associate. He liked to say that he was learning to cook here. He even washed his own clothes and found time for everything.

His family and friends sent him numerous letters, cards, books and messages. He wrote back, saying: "Many thanks for the company of your prayers and correspondence; I have tried to answer all of you who have written; if someone has not received an answer from me, it is because of Kenya's postal system." He showed his faithfulness to his friends by all these small details and said to me that for him, writing to all his friends and acquaintances was a ministry in itself.

An extraordinary man

He was an extraordinary individual, an intellectual, polyglot, theologian, writer, educator, servant of the people, and great communicator. His constant focus was a continual search to live a life in complete harmony with the teachings of Jesus Christ, among the poor and marginalized; to build a Church-community centered around the person of Jesus Christ, and bereft of all display of fame, riches or power. The spirituality of the Priests of the Prado - a French order dedicated to working with the poor - had left its mark on him, and was of comfort in difficult times.

He was a voracious reader, not only during the day, but often until midnight. His critical sense and wisdom were a great incentive to our team. He had comments for us on all the books he had read and would invite us to read them also, including many of the letters and articles received from family and friends.

His testimony, his preoccupation with the infirm, poor and elderly, his smile and greetings for everyone, his daily efforts to preach in and speak the vernacular, his human warmth and intuition, his simplicity in living according to the gospel, this and much more, reads as a litany, and is the seed that Carlos has sown among us. The Samburu referred to him as, *Carlos, Ololmunyei, Lpadri oata nkosheke naibor*. (Carlos, with the beard, the father with the white stomach. Their way of saying "with a kind heart.") He really enjoyed his stay at the mission, without expecting to play a prominent role. He lived a happy life and often said the best thing in his life was to have come to Africa.

In a 1995 Christmas card, he wrote: "These shepherds are peaceful, quiet, smiling men and women; when we go by in the mission Jeep, the only vehicle traveling through, they immediately come out to regale us with their smiles, which are refreshing to us. They are well-defined and transparent smiles, precisely because they come from men and women whose lives center around very little, the minimum necessary for survival. They carry little baggage with them in life, an uncontaminated existence in which they retain all things that offer permanent contact with nature, the animals, the sun, moon and stars. If the shepherds of Bethlehem were like this, then I can understand why they were the first to receive the news of Jesus' birth; I also understand why they were the first to approach the manger.

It is here in the Samburu semi-desert where I have enjoyed the evening stars for the first time. From our mission terrace we can contemplate them almost every night. Nothing new happens in the pastoral world because everything is new! Life is lived by enjoying what is normal, the ordinary; happiness and joy do not come from the extraordinary; nor do possessions produce these feelings. They come from fascination with the commonplace. One never sees these young shepherds and shepherdesses bored, as if carrying a heavy weight, or loaded down with work. Their herds are their happiness; the only source of income at the peak of their lives."

The final days

We were able to live out Carlos Alberto's last days in faith's light. He lived an awareness of Christ's death and resurrection, and soon began to have a premonition of his own death, which he accepted as something normal.

On Ash Wednesday, he very assiduously conducted the blessings with ashes in the dual communities of Suyian and Loilei. On February 21, after celebrating the opening ceremonies of Lent in Suyian, he went to perform them again for the local people of Loilei, accompanied by the mission's male-nurse. He sleeps in a *manyata*, visits with the nearby residents and shares with them the little food he has brought along. This is a place hard hit by the drought; not a drop of rain has fallen since the end of December. On Friday the 23rd, he returns to the mission, and after lunch takes his customary sacred nap and says that he is feeling a little tired. On Saturday, he rests and then writes, continuing to fill his notebook with notes. On Sunday, the 25th, he celebrates the Eucharist at the mission along with Father Juan Carlos.

When I returned that afternoon, we left for our monthly retreat and planning meeting. Carlos drove the car, slowly and carefully, as he usually did. Our vehicle was old, and the roads, rough. We didn't quite make it to the meeting place, thanks to a mechanical problem. We put the car in four-wheel drive and started back, hoping to spend the night at Wamba. But it was impossible to get through an impromptu lake, one of the sandy rivers that suddenly fills with water during the rainy season, and consequently were forced to sleep in the car.

The following morning, Father Juan Carlos and I set out looking for help and hoping to secure some food. We returned a little before 9:00 AM, in the company of several adults, and with some warm tea for Carlos, who was sleeping comfortably. With the Samburus' help, we got the car moving and headed for Wamba, intending to take it to be repaired. While at Wamba, we visited the sick. Carlos Alberto spoke to one of the nuns in regard to a young girl who had slipped into a coma. The child was from our mission, and only a few days earlier, he had driven her to the hospital. Carlos Alberto was telling the nun that the girl deserved to die with dignity and that they should please not prolong her life uselessly. Then we talked about the various artificial means utilized to prolong life and his reasons for being opposed to them. He had already expressed in a letter his wish that such artificial methods not be used if he were critically ill.

On Monday he celebrated the sacrament of reconciliation with the pastor at Wamba, Father Vioto. On the morning of March 27, Father Genaro Ardila, a Colombian member of La Consolata - an Italian missionary organization - who was working in Wamba, took us back to our mission. We agreed to return on our motorcycle that coming weekend, in order to pick up our car once it was fixed.

Illness and suffering

On the morning of Wednesday the 28th, Carlos was visiting with the people of Barsaloi, trying to get them interested in the meeting of Christians that afternoon. He was with one of the small communities of beginners.

When he returned, he stated that he was not feeling well and was experiencing chills to some degree. Nevertheless, he kept reading for some time. After prayer, we went out to eat, but he complained of lack of appetite, wishing only to try a little something and then go to bed immediately. We thought that he might be experiencing his first encounter with malaria, a scourge we had all gone through. Between nine and ten that evening, we stayed with him, for he had a temperature of 38 and 39 degrees (100 -101 F).

We placed some fresh water and a clean towel in his room. Then, that night, he wrote a letter of goodbye to all of us. On thursday the 29th, he said that he had not had a good night and was not feeling well, even though his fever was a little lower. We didn't have a car to take him to Wamba, but miraculously one arrived at the mission in search of water. In it was a group belonging to an NGO. When I explained to them the seriousness of my mission colleague's illness, they finally replied at about 3:30 in the afternoon, that they would be able to take Carlos

Alberto to the hospital. Nevertheless, he asked that they wait until that Friday morning, for it was a little late, and feeling somewhat better, he was making out the payroll for the employees. In spite of our urging, he kept insisting that Friday would be better. I was ready to go with him, but it was impossible to convince him that it was absolutely necessary to leave at once. That night, his fever rose to 39 degrees (101 F).

On Friday, March 1, I went to his room a little before six in the morning. He had already bathed, and said that he was not feeling well. The NGO car came back for him, and in less than an hour and fifty minutes we were at the hospital in Wamba. When we arrived, he complained of feeling very ill and could foresee that he was going to die. The vomiting had stopped a little, and he was able to get out of the car and walk, clearly aware of what was going on. The doctor examined him and immediately informed us the priest was suffering from malaria. They gave him a saline solution, but the blood tests for malaria proved to be negative.

I remained with him all that afternoon, noting that he was semi-conscious. Then suddenly he asked me where the driver of the car was, for he wanted to thank him. Two male nurses, a doctor and the nuns cared for him continually. His temperature had stabilized at 37 degrees (100 F).

By seven o'clock that evening, he was resting comfortably. At about nine o'clock, I went to see him and he told me that he felt a little better but that the malaria was pretty severe. I asked him if I could get him anything, and he said, "a little water, but later." We said goodbye to one another. At 9:15, one of the Sisters entered his room. Carlos requested a blanket and told her he was feeling very ill. His fever had risen to 40 degrees (104 F), in a short time. The doctors, nuns and male nurses were at his bedside, administering oxygen and applying ice to various parts of his body. Carlos Alberto slipped into a coma, near death.

They called me at the mission, and when I arrived, I could see that he was critical. His temperature was 42.4 degrees (over 105 F), and the medical staff was trying everything possible to save him. The attending physician, Doctor Prandoni, explained that it was a serious case of cerebral malaria. Yet, the blood tests continued to be negative.

Father Vioto, the mission pastor, administered the sacrament of the Anointing of the Sick. Right before midnight, I communicated with Nairobi by radiotelephone, in order to notify our superior, Father Jairo Gómez, how serious Carlos Alberto was. We considered the possibility of transporting him to the capital in a small aircraft.

By two in the morning, they had succeeded in controlling his fever a little. I went to his room and spoke to him; he signaled me that he could hear me. At six o'clock, they summoned me to his room again to say that his condition had worsened. He was bleeding internally, and his fever was still very high. I felt that his final hour was drawing near.

The rain had returned ferociously that morning, after a pause of several months. I was able to communicate with Father Jairo at eight o'clock and relayed how serious Carlos' condition was. He replied that the Flying Doctors were awaiting the attending physician's authorization to transport him to the intensive care unit in Nairobi. The female doctor, an Italian national in charge of the Wamba hospital, said Carlos Alberto could not survive the trip at that time, since his blood pressure was very low. At ten in the morning, the authorization for the trip arrived. At eleven thirty the small aircraft landed at Wamba, and in less than an hour, we were at the Nairobi airport where an ambulance awaited us, and within thirty minutes they were caring for the patient in the clinic.

The internal hemorrhaging was very serious. Donations of blood were administered immediately, but pneumonia set in and there were slight kidney complications. On Thursday, March 7, his sister Gloria arrived from London. He remained in critical condition, even as they performed renal dialysis for several days. Gloria's husband Mauricio, who was specializing in medicine, also arrived from London.

In truth, Carlos Alberto was already clinically dead, and if some of the attending doctors lacked complete honesty, they would be prolonging his life solely for economic gain. A brain scan showed severe cerebral damage. On Monday the 25th, we agreed to respect the right to die with dignity that Carlos had signed and had always defended. His sister and brother-in-law asked the doctor to remove the life-sustaining machines and he was then taken to a special-care unit.

A great surprise

On Tuesday, March 26, after having been informed by telephone of the seriousness of our beloved Carlos, I went to his room in Barsaloi to pick up the mail he had recently received, in order to give it to Gloria. To my amazement, I found his letter of goodbye in one of the notebooks where he did his Kisamburu language exercises. This left a great impression on me, and after an hour of praying, I realized that a mystic experience of our brother had transpired on that Wednesday, the 28th of February, when fever had overcome his entire body.

I felt I had to share that page with my mission colleague, Father Jairo Valbuena, who was also deeply moved by it. The following morning we undertook our long voyage to Nairobi, for we knew that Carlos Alberto was about to die. After twelve hours of travel, we arrived at our house in the capital. The next day we celebrated a Mass, attended by Gloria, Carlos' sister, and all of the Yarumal Missionary team in Kenya. As I began the ritual, I stated that I had something important to share with everyone during the homily. Then, in an atmosphere of prayer, I read Carlos' farewell letter:

2/28/96

"A night with a full-moon, in the Samburu desert! The Ilakir (eyes) of Enkai (God) have gone into hiding. Welcome sister death! My fever is rising intensely, there is no possibility of going to the hospital at Wamba. As usual, our Toyota is not running.

I feel a great force, happy in the face of death. I have lived passionately my love for humanity and for Jesus' plan. I am dying completely happy. I committed some mistakes, made people suffer. I hope they will forgive me! How wonderful it is to die like the poorest and most marginal! Without any chance of getting to the hospital. How nice if no one were to die this way any more, I hope all of you will promise me this!
A fervent embrace of love for all, both men and women."

Carlos Alberto

ILAKIR: *The stars. For the Samburu, they are the eyes of Nkai with which he watches over the trees, rivers, flowers, pasture, land and cattle, at night, so that we humans can rest undisturbed.*

NKAI: *God of the Samburu and Masai. The Kikuyos, the largest of Kenya's tribes, call him Ngai. It is the first name used to refer to the Creator, who curiously, is not masculine, but feminine in gender. It is not that, for them, God is a woman. God is neither male nor female. God is simply God. In their way of thinking, this is equivalent to saying that God has meaning in itself. Nkai is the source of fruitfulness and fertility, the unending source of life.*

After the reading of Carlos Alberto's letter, we all understood his passage from death to life, for which he was already prepared.

During that week, we visited him constantly in the hospital. Saturday, March 30, on the Eve of Palm Sunday, we traveled to our respective missions to be with our people during Holy Week. Since our companion's death was a foregone conclusion, we agreed that if he were to die during Holy Week, we would celebrate the funeral on Easter, when all of us had returned. We also wanted to move Carlos Alberto to our residence in order to care for him during his last days.

Sister Death

At Barsaloi, we received the news of the state of our companion's health, during the week. But on Wednesday, the 3rd, our telephone stopped working and we were incommunicado.

On Good Friday, April 5, at three in the afternoon, Carlos Alberto returned to the house of the Father, after having been in a coma for one month. We understood the special meaning of that time and day.

On Sunday morning, while I was celebrating the Mass of the Lord's Resurrection for the Christian community of Barsaloi, Father Genaro Ardila arrived from Wamba, to tell me the news of Carlos Alberto's death. Greatly saddened, but full of hope, I immediately communicated the news to the entire Christian community. A great silence overcame the church, while many tears flowed. Then we sang the Hallelujah of the Resurrection. The next day, early Monday morning, we traveled to Nairobi to celebrate the funeral of our priest and friend. A few mechanical problems with the car complicated things a little, but in the end, we were all together in the capital, the whole team and numerous friends.

The funeral was scheduled for Wednesday, April 10, in the chapel of Hekima College, run by Jesuit fathers, and where our seminarians study their theology. A large gathering of bishops, priests, sisters and members of the Christian community accompanied us with their prayers at the death and resurrection of our brother.

Our regional director, Father Jairo Gómez, presided over the moving farewell to our priest and friend. After the funeral ceremony, his body was transferred to the cremation site. Gloria Calderón, Carlos Alberto's sister, was entrusted with the task of transporting the ashes from Eastern Africa to the Colombian city of Medellín, where days later a final farewell was given to this outstanding priest, in an emotional, jam-packed Mass, celebrated by Monsignor Hector Rueda Hernández, priest from the Archdiocese of Medellín, and attended by numerous friends.

Those of us who were able to experience first-hand Carlos Alberto's Christian missionary testimony -a ministry intensely lived- his joy and intuition, his extraordinary values, and who shared his friendship, must admit that he was an unforgettable individual, an immensely human priest. He loved God and people deeply. In death, he continues to enlighten and sustain our arduous task among the Samburu.

CHRIST IS OUR LIFE

Jesus Christ is the basis of our faith. He is the reason for which we have come to Africa in order to spend our lives in Primary Evangelization among the poor. The death of Carlos Alberto strengthened our commitment to go on. His unseen presence continues to aid us in ministering to those whom the world considers to be insignificant. But God's Word reassures us that the Kingdom of Heaven belongs to them, the marginalized.

An eternal memory

This could very well have been the reason our mission companion, Father Carlos Alberto Calderón was inspired to devote his life, and offer it unconditionally, to serving the poor and marginalized.

He could never have imagined that the Lord would call on a Good Friday, summoning him from a faraway country of Eastern Africa, at a great distance from his homeland. It is certain that the how and why of his death were immaterial to him, for he had always surrendered to the will of Jesus Christ, unselfishly and with trust.

The "preparations for dying," his mystical experience, and death on Good Friday, are signs that, taken from the perspective of faith, somewhat reveal to us God's mystery and actions in the person of Carlos Alberto. Time will possibly help us to better understand and evaluate the testimony of this great missionary.

He was admired by many, though controversial, and always asking "why?" A scholarly priest in sociology and theology, he was among the most committed to the cause of the poor and marginalized. Intellectually gifted, he was known in many places of Latin America and Europe where he had been invited to talk, lecture and conduct retreats. He was a friend of many of the proponents of Liberation Theology, with whom he also shared a love for Jesus Christ and His Word.

His daring decision to go to Brazil, at the invitation of Monsignor Helder Camara, in order to determine the direction of diocesan priestly retreats, caused some friction with the then-Archbishop of Medellín, Colombia. Threatened with death by the powerful landowners, Carlos Alberto was forced to seek refuge on the other side of the planet, far from his homeland.

Upon returning to his native archdiocese, he began to teach again at the university that had revoked his professorship, and to work among the poorest of the poor. One day in 1994, two months after his mother's death, he decided to serve as a missionary in Africa, joining the Missionaries of Yarumal. One of the bishops advised the popular priest not to follow through with the decision. "How can you leave now that you are in your finest hour? Everyone knows you and holds you in high esteem; you are important to us, and we can give you a promotion," the bishop said.

"That is exactly why I want to leave, because I want to live the Gospel more faithfully," was Father Calderón's reply.

Carlos Alberto truly understood that the Church is entirely missionary, and that the call to go beyond one's borders is not only a vocation and the responsibility of all missionary institutions, but that diocesan priests can also receive the call to serve outside their diocesan limits; for bishops should be shepherds, less limited in outlook, and more universal.

After a little more than a year on African soil, he was to write to a friend: "The richness of the life I am living exceeds all expectations I had when I made the decision to come here. For that reason, I can truly do nothing other than to thank God and this life for the gift I am being given by this experience. Though this life is not without its difficulties, problems, and preoccupations, it is the awareness that life is being lived alongside forgotten men and women, both economically and politically insignificant, that makes this experience so meaningful. Jesus said, 'He who loves his life, loses it; and he who hates his life in this world, keeps it unto life everlasting'"(John 12 :25).

Together with our mission people, we will celebrate the death and resurrection of our companion and friend, Father Carlos Alberto Calderón. His far-away presence gives more meaning to our stay among the tribe he loved so much, and with whom he spent his last moments in our midst. April 5th, is a day on which we must give thanks to God, and reaffirm our faith in the Resurrected Christ.

THE SEARCH FOR TRACES
OF CARLOS ALBERTO

In February of 1998, Dr. Gloria Cuartas, former mayor of the Colombian city of Apartadó, visited us at the mission in Barsaloi. Small in stature, but with a heart exuding the dream of peace, she braved these rough paths, in pursuit of traces of Carlos Alberto and the source of happiness of the man they still remembered.

In contrast to the majority of tourists, businessmen who come to Africa for a safari, Gloria preferred to share her time with the poor in order to experience a different reality of this continent. After taking part in an encounter for women, in Ruanda, sponsored by the United Nations, she came to Kenya, anxious to learn where Carlos Alberto had spent the last few months of his life.

The Testimony

She, herself, tells us why she has searched for those of us who took part in that religious brother's heroic missionary adventure:

I have followed this path with great joy, placing my hopes in a traveling Jesus, to guide us along the paths followed by many of the marginal, who are burdened with loneliness. But always in the same place, his love is present throughout nature, and in mother earth.

For that reason, I felt in my heart that some day I would come to this travelers' place and felt that someone was telling me love is a generous gift to the humble, and without knowing it, Father Carlos Alberto Calderón also helped me to follow my own path. He was the reason I was inspired to come here. Upon my arrival, I find a mission working to introduce the Gospel, and I have seen you, the Yarumal Missionaries, live a life of service, in search of justice. Here, in this remote land of Barsaloi, you proclaim the Good News to your young people; it is an unmistakable reality building a new day in the active presence of Jesus the shepherd, along with the lowly, hard-working, marginalized Mary.

134

You are without scheduled hours, Saturdays or Sundays free, and lacking the comforts of modern life; but I sensed that you are rekindling hope and educating in love, in tenderness, and that the gospel of freedom will become real. The task is a long one, but has already begun.

I thank you for showing me a new way to live in love; you have allowed me to become happy. Accompanying me is the happiness of the entire Colombian missionary team making its presence known in this part of the African continent; I have learned from the serenity and the silence, the same things I saw in the shepherds and shepherdesses; in their smiles, the only means of communication among us, in my case. I also felt the simplicity in the midst of nature's desolation, in the same way.

Everything is part of the universe, of nature, a collection of beauty, where all languages are spoken, and also where the call is heard to raise the poor out of their marginal existence.

I think that your experience in this environment of Primary Evangelization contributes to, hopefully, many professionals succeeding in understanding their role in the globalization process. How nice it would be, if many of us could understand, despite the distances, that there are in existence human beings and developing cultures in a world that still maintain their purity, almost in defiance of living a totally different reality.

You, the missionaries, have seen in the people, a live Jesus. You see Him in their sorrow, and in their traditions. All of this is a way of informing people, who today are in search of other adventures and who, like me, feel that life cannot pass us by unnoticed. For it is urgent that we begin a move toward a kind of justice, that will permit us to live in the midst of this global village.

Thank you for living among the most needy and speaking their language, all of which makes us more human and closer to the love of God.

The intention of the program for the evangelization of Jesus is to introduce the unfamiliar Gospel, through word, life, and testimony, without violating the culture and true spirituality of other peoples. Easter celebration in Suyian.

One never sees these young shepherds and shepherdesses bored or as if carrying a heavy weight on their shoulders, or loaded down with work. Their herds are their happiness, the only source of income at the peak of their lives.

Part

THREE

PROFILE OF A PRIMARY EVANGELIZATION MISSIONARY

1) A man of God

A person who undertakes the task of Primary Evangelization must possess deep faith in the living body of Jesus Christ. He must be fully aware of his assignment, willing to find God in each person and all cultures. He must be a man of prayer and contemplation, a firm believer in God.

2) Someone of open mind and heart

Free of fanaticism, willing to understand and appreciate different cultures, without passing judgment, nor spreading prejudice from his own formative surroundings. He must be open to the universe, with a heart big enough to encompass the entire cosmos.

3) Someone eminently human

He must love people and be comfortable with his new brothers and sisters. He must be sensitive to the joys and sorrows of those with whom he shares life, being a part of their ceremonies and community activities.

4) A scholar

He must be willing to grow intellectually, a lover of the culture and language of the area to which he is assigned. He must also possess the gift of an investigative mind in order to delve deeper into the seemingly obvious. He must be a constant observer of the signs and symbols of the new culture he shares, and able to invent new methods in teaching and introducing the word of God. He must value research.

5) An untiring team-member

Primary evangelization is accomplished by team effort, or it is not achieved at all. In the new cultural environment it is necessary to share with a colleague, the celebrations, pardons, evaluations, planning, prayers, studying and rest. Individual and group testimonies are indispensable to the message's credibility. When a missionary team is brimming with happiness, and responsibility is shared, everything will proceed well.

6) An unswerving witness to God's love

He must make a daily effort to be true to the faith he preaches. God loves all of us equally, having given us the gift of his Son, Jesus, and the strength of his Holy Spirit. Introducing the living body of Jesus, in all its magnitude, must be the core of all catechesis and the focal point of every religious celebration.

7) A man of undying hope

Evangelization is a slow process; that is to say, it must be carried out slowly, without the expectation of immediate results. Then, the evangelizing missionary will be content to simply be present. He will learn to remain silent, listen, enjoy, and allow himself to be taught by others. By assuming an attitude of sincere respect, he will be able to understand the people's progression. He must be constant in his task, and forever optimistic, for after all, it is God who will bring about the change.

8) Kind, but not paternalistic

He will be careful to promote the values of the culture he has come to, before becoming a giver of things. He will not create artificial needs for these human groups, and even less, establish dependencies. By living a simple life, he will become the friend of everyone, taking care not to show preferences among people; that is, acting fatherly, without becoming paternalistic.

9) Someone able to trust and delegate

He will get to know community leaders, in order to evaluate and consult them. He will rely on the efforts of the laity, catechists and other workers associated with the pastoral mission. He will be familiar with the experiences of others involved in primary evangelization on local, regional, diocesan, national and international levels. He will allow the people to help plan and will make them partially responsible for all procedures. He will have faith in his fellow people.

10)   A Christian defender of life at all cost

The Gospel is Good News, and Jesus came, "that they may have life, and have it more abundantly (John 10 :10)". The missionary will be an invincible defender of life. He will support all measures promoting dignity and human rights. Since in every culture there are situations or organizations that go against life, he will denounce the violation of those rights and all instances of injustice, violence and oppression, as a proclaimer of the truth.

Night begins to fall. The smile of young shepherds and the gracious dancing young girl, invite one to live in this African world full of mystery and passion. These young shepherdesses have felt quite welcome by us and have found a place in the Church. The vast majority of them speak only Samburu. Hearing our sermons and prayers in their own language makes them feel that the Church is also theirs.

PRIMARY EVANGELIZATION METHODOLOGY

ecause each situation is different, there is no one method suitable for evangelizing in disparate cultures.

It is not the same presenting the living body of Jesus to a sedentary, agricultural or piscatorial tribe, as it would be to a semi-nomadic, pastoral people. That being the case, I would like to share the guidelines for our evangelization mission among the Samburu of Kenya. Our program is as follows:

1) A slow process of introduction -concrete representation- inculturation
- A knowledge of the reality, history and world view of the groups we are serving.
- Respect for the people and their culture.
- Learning the local language.
- Adapting to a new way of life.

2) Teamwork and a life of testimony
- Be mindful that primary evangelization is carried out by teamwork, or not at all.
- Pray individually and in groups, as prayer fuels our labor. Share, celebrate, plan, evaluate, study, pardon, and rest, together.
- Be a sign of and witness to Christian life for the people with whom we live.
- Experience God's love inside missionary brotherhoods, trying to live what we preach.

3) Interfaith dialogue
- Know and appreciate the faith of others.
- Recognize and value the seeds of the Word, that have taken root in all cultures, through God's love, which encompasses all His children.
- Avoid all fanatical ideas, in your heart and in your actions.
- Don't judge the other culture, its faith, practices and celebrations by your personal standards.
- Learn about each religion and faith with simplicity, to enrich your faith in Jesus Christ.

141

4) Present the living Christ and His basic values in a friendly, simple and disinterested way

- Visit the people. Share with them, get to know them and get them to know us.
- Create bonds of friendship, through sincere and open contact.
- Offer them directly the living Jesus, by inviting them to pray and to know him, remaining mindful of the fact that this open offer may be refused.
- Accompany, motivate and share with these listeners the Word of God.
- Answer the people's questions, stimulate their interest and responsibly prepare what is to be shared at each meeting.

5) Beginning the catechization

- After a period of time as participants in a group listening to the Word, allow the people to ask, to feel the necessity, desire, or the call to choose following Jesus Christ in the Church.
- Kerygma-introduction. Deep portrayal of the living Jesus. Our faith, the Church signs, symbols. The Bible.
- Duration and intensity according to the circumstances of the catechization.
- Joyful celebration of the faith in all its aspects and experiences.

6) Promote the growth of each community according to Christ the model for humanity

- Accompany the new Christians in the growth of their faith.
- Pray, celebrate, meditate on the Word of God, together.
- Share responsibilities with members of the community.
- Stimulate and support life's obligations according to the Word of God.
- Awaken a missionary consciousness in the small community.
- Analyze, read, reflect and act on the reality of the life being lived.

7) Community members as a preeminent evangelization force

- Promote, shape and empower community leaders.
- Local catechist schools. (Avoid payment to these catechists, as many would study for economic reasons, rather than in pursuit of a vocation).
- Share responsibilities and roles during the various activities.
- Rely upon a "parish" council of laymen.
- Engage in dialogue, support, formation and motivation, with religion teachers.
- Consult, share, analyze, and make decisions with the assistance of community leaders or "experts."
- Plan, schedule and evaluate with lay participation.

8) The nascent church must be a missionary one

- Create in the Christians a consciousness of their missionary vocation.

- Share the faith with other Christians or announce it to the non-Christians.
- Promote, participate in and devise courses and missionary activities on local, diocesan and national levels.
- Invite and promote local vocations.
- Without demonstrating instability, be conscious of our itinerant condition, and of the fact that we must promote the growth of a local Church so that it may become completely self-sufficient as well as missionary in scope.

9) **Promoting the plenitude of life**
- Uphold and value all personal and community efforts in support of life.
- Promote justice, freedom and peace.
- Analyze the local and national situations, and denounce openly any move against life.
- Search for satisfactory solutions (cooperatives, development groups, health projects, housing, employment) on a local or external level, while avoiding paternalism and dependency.
- Champion equality of the sexes, and support preparation, training and advancement.

10) **Study and lasting preparation**
- The need to energize oneself through enduring training, and individual and group studies.
- Live in harmony with the signs of the times.
- Participate in courses, seminars, meetings, and personal and group retreats.
- Evaluate methodology and promote new techniques.
- Articulate and share with the community and others, if possible, the missionary experience, how God is experienced in other cultures.
- Collect, organize and systematize the missionary experience of different teams and missionary brotherhoods, sharing this information with the entire community.

In our East African missionary experiment, we believe that we have made progress, and have tried to follow this plan of instruction.

Our mission centers, among the Kipsigis and Samburu, present very distinct situations and varied procedures.

The Kipsigui are moving from a semi-nomadic existence to a sedentary and agricultural life. Their religious instruction began more than half a century ago in some places and they are progressing in this process of primary evangelization, through very positive experiences in some communities; yet, there are closed groups where advances have not been made or simply stated, the Good News of Jesus Christ has not been accepted, and therefore the people continue to practice their traditional religion. Due to the maturation of the faith in other communities, there is a rise of new local vocations, and leaders, indicating to foreign missionaries that it is time to introduce those areas to the local clergy. This has been the impetus for opening a mission post in Ethiopia.

"I will lead her to the wilderness and I will speak to her heart," (Hos. 2 :16). When we assume a desert-like posture, we must humbly present ourselves before the Lord, *"Speak, Lord, for thy servant heareth,"* (1 Sam. 3 :9). In the face of all the unexpected events that occur in life, God continues to appear as our guide, leading, supporting and calling. In the desert, we encounter God, as we reflect on his most unpretentious beings.

A CHRISTIAN SENSE OF THE DESERT

Introduction

Leaving our native environment, abandoning the surroundings in which we were born and raised —for many of us, fertile lands colored by various shades of greenness, trees, and flowers, whether small town or city— and moving to the desert, where sand, rocks, savage beasts, and a dearth of water are the distinguishing characteristics, is frightening as well as impressive.

This pilgrimage entails going from the known to the unknown, leaving behind loved ones while in search of others, abandoning the comforts, hustle and bustle of a crowded area, and entering into a world of simplicity, silence and solitude.

The desert has many redeeming qualities. A person does not venture there out of initiative or in search of adventure. It is God who leads one there. We are told so by Abraham, the ancient prophets, John the Baptist, and Jesus himself. By means of the desert, God puts them on the path to something new, the fulfillment of his great promises. This also happens to Jesus, when the Holy Spirit directs him into the desert, prior to the start of his preaching.

It is God who provides the initiative, by means of the first manifestation, a calling. The believer does not follow this path on his own, nor desire it as an escape. The whole process is enveloped in mystery. It is God's teaching that reveals itself to us, taking us to a point of conversion and acceptance of a specific mission.

The experience of God in the desert has several stages, which at times seem illogical, by reason of their contrasts. The desert is life and death, solitude and company, aridness and oasis, temptation and freedom. The desert conquers pride and dispels arrogance. It lays bare our smallness; it distances us from false appearances and causes us to focus on the essential: Jesus Christ and his Gospel. It fills us with the Spirit of God.

In our journey of brotherhood, we live this desert experience and God, in a constant cyclical relationship. God - us - me - the others - the universal Church - nature - signs of the times - God. God's word is our light and our source of information. The people with whom we share life are our teachers, our inspirational figures. The desert, therefore, consists of:

1) Experiencing death in the desert

In many biblical passages, we see the desert as a dangerous, desolate place, dominated by the forces of evil (Dt. 8 :15; Num. 21 :4-9; Is. 30 :6). At first glance, the desert does inspire terror, a fear resulting from many years of deforestation and being a place of death. The desert is often interpreted as remoteness from God (Is. 6 :11; 54 :3; Jer. 4 :7; Ez. 26 :19), and the triumph of the devil's powers. It is also a kingdom of the dead (Ez. 34 :25). According to Luke 11 :24, evil spirits live there, in a region of temptation and damnation, an isolated area where one can lose both life and identity.

Living in the desert means being away from home and in danger (Acts. 1 :18-20; Mt. 12 :43; Mk. 1 :12).

Isolation, hunger, thirst, undernourishment, illnesses such as malaria, enemy attacks, premature death and the indifference of a central government are very real daily experiences for those of us who have come to the desert.

Upon crossing the desert, the prophet Elijah feels exhausted and distressed, wishing to die (1 Kgs. 19 :1-7). Our experience in the desert has been marked with similar signs of desperation, out of powerlessness in the face of human suffering and defeated by injustice and lack of solidarity; we feel inadequate before the magnitude of our problems.

One of our mission colleagues gave up his life, a victim of cerebral malaria. On various occasions, the attackers have come as far as our mission armed with modern weapons, and have killed many people, while stealing their cattle. Powerless, we have thought about the children and young people who die from malaria and other illnesses that could have been wiped out. We have suffered with the pregnant women who lost their lives -some, while riding in the mission vehicle, on route to the hospital-.

The routine periods of drought cause the shepherds great pain, often resulting in the loss of their lives and livestock. At times troubled, we ask ourselves, "Why do our tribes continue to live at length in such arid surroundings?"

Facing impending death or severe illness, the Samburu pray to their God, Nkai, the following words: *Nkai ai, mikiya nimikiar, njooki ake maituyo nkishon, njooki matibiko adol Itorrok o supati* (Oh my God, don't take me away, and don't kill me; give me the joy of a long life; permit me to remain and distinguish between good and evil).

146

2) Experiencing crisis in the desert

God said to Abraham, "Leave your country, your kinsfolk, and your father's house, for the land I will show you" (Gen. 12 :1). Any severance or search for something new, brings with it a crisis, and experience shows us that only by facing a crisis can we grow in maturity. There is an African proverb that states, "Laughter and tears go side by side."

In order to restore the lost garden of Eden, Jesus crossed the desert. After hearing the voice from heaven stating, "This is my Beloved Son, he was led into the desert by the Spirit, to be tempted by the devil" (Mt. 4 :1).

The people of Israel had already suffered severe crises during their crossing of the desert, without water or food. And they therefore began to long for their life of slavery (Ex. 17 :1-7).

Beginning a new life, opening oneself up to new values, customs, expressions, language, symbols and signs, is not an easy task. Crises arise when we least expect them. Some people give in to the cultural shock and all of its new ways, and decide to return to the familiar homeland to speak their native language, to enjoy the company of loved ones, eat the foods they are accustomed to eating, and to relish in the comforts lacking in the desert.

To live here is tantamount to danger, especially from an environmental point of view. In this region, there are thorns everywhere; more than ninety-five percent of the trees and bushes have thorns. Driving a car or motorcycle on roads of sand is a real adventure, and many nights are spent out in the open. It also means traveling long days, to avoid danger. Wild beasts roam many regions.

Before each trip, preparations must be made: Potable water, some food, lanterns, matches, knife or machete, and indispensable emergency tools.

Though an intrinsic part of the human condition, we tend to reject temptation and suffering. We know that God's Spirit is involved. Saint Paul lists all the crises he has overcome and feels guided by the Lord (1 Cor. 4 :7-12).

When a woman gives birth, or someone suffers a moment of crisis, the Samburu intone the following prayer: *Ashe naa Nkai, itishe te serian, incoo iyioo matodol likae apa ng'ejuk.* ("Thank you my Lord, I have given birth peaceully, grant us the sight of another new moon").

3) The desert, an experience in solitude

The desert is by nature a lonely place. At the end of a long voyage, one is finally there, where sand dunes and rocks are limitless, and daytime heat contrasts greatly with the chill of the night.

But solitude is a special place for prayer, where one can abandon oneself completely to the Father's hands. In the desert solitude means the relinquishment of everything, a suitable place for a prophetic outcry, evidence of a calling, infinite tension, inner peace, confrontation with oneself.

When coming into contact with the desert inhabitants, we must learn their language in order to unravel the mysteries of their culture. The lack of understanding, not being able to communicate, plunges us into a torturous loneliness. We become children again, enmeshed in complete helplessness, unable to lead.

Learning a new language is a source of hardship as well as satisfaction. It is an effort that sharpens one's will, and later provides many rewards. Israel found its salvation in the desert (Ez. 34 :25; Hos. 2 :16). In solitude, God reveals himself to us. Though it is impossible for many people to go to a physical desert, we may procure a spiritual ground inside of us in order to engage in intimate communication with the Creator. Jesus said, "I am with you all days, even unto the consummation of the world" (Mt. 28 :18-20). A relationship with God, at times, increases amid struggle and temptation.

The Samburu people discover God's presence at every moment and in every place; therefore they frequently say: *Ketaana Nkai oleng kake mikindim aatodol. Kore nikidolie naa asat naitaas iyioo nkata pooki kwarie e parkiji o nkata e mayian,* ("God is very near, but we are incapable of seeing him. What we see are the things He is accustomed to do for us at any moment, night or day, or during a blessing.").

4) The desert, an experience in freedom

The wandering through the desert of the people of Israel for more than forty years was understood to be a prime example of liberation and was recalled each year during the Easter celebration (Ex. 15 :22 to 18 :27). Israel's long journey through the desert prepared it for receiving the promised land.

John begins to preach in the desert (Mt. 3 :1-3; Lk. 3 :1). He is entrusted with preparing the way for the Savior. No other prophet like him spoke with signs and words. "A voice clamors forth in the desert," and his cry invites people to convert in order to free themselves from sin.

Listening to the Word of God, and living it, can free us from an oppressive false sense of security.

It was precisely in the desert where the Word of God came to John, a solitary, austere man, always removed from the centers of power. His word was a liberating wind, and purifying fire. "Make ready the way of the Lord" (Mt. 3 :3).

Jesus, the new Moses (Hab. 3 :22), accompanies his parents to Egypt, and from there is called by God (Mt. 2). We all need to surrender ourselves to obedience of the Spirit in order to be led to the desert, leaving the confines of a comfortable home and a more secure temple.

For the Samburu, the source of their wealth and happiness lies in their children and their cattle, and for that reason they pray to Nkai, saying: "*Nkai ai, ingilunye iyioo nkishon ino ee nkera o noo swom*", ("My God, surround us with your life, all our children and cattle").

5) The desert, experiencing God

"I will lead her to the wilderness and I will speak to her heart" (Os. 2 :16). In the desert, the people of Israel discover the presence of God openly. There the Lord appears through diverse theophanies such as the flaming bush (Ex. 3 :1), and the soft breeze of Elijah (1 Kgs. 19 :11-18). The wandering of the people of Israel through the desert explains the close proximity of God to his people (Hos. 9 :10), through trials and infidelity.

When we assume a desert-like posture, we must humbly present ourselves before the Lord, "Speak, Lord, for your servant listens" (1 Sam. 3 :9).

A posture of abandonment in the desert led brother Carlos de Foucault to pray, giving himself up completely to God: "Father, I place myself in your hands. Do with me as you choose. I shall be grateful to you for what you do with me. I am ready for anything, provided your will be done in me and in all your creatures. I wish for nothing more, my God. Place my soul in your hands. I give it to you, my God, with all the love in my heart, for I love you, and because I believe loving you is to give myself up, surrender myself unconditionally, with boundless trust, for You are my Father."

God reveals his true identity in the desert. "I am who I am" (Ex. 3 :14), he tells Moses. The desert is a theological place. In the face of so many uncertainties surrounding us in life, God continues to act as a guide, a leader who sustains and calls us.

Our experience in encountering and speaking with God through individual prayer and the missionary brotherhood, continues to show us quite clearly how the Lord protects, accompanies, and strengthens us with his abounding goodness and presence. In the desert we are able to perceive more precisely the figure of God and feel loved by Him, in our insignificance.

The vastness of the desert is well suited to praising and blessing the Creator. "O Lord, our Lord, how glorious is your name over all the earth" (Ps. 8). If many people are anxious to contemplate the God of creation and his greatness, the desert is a suitable place. Here, one can enjoy an azure sky free from pollution, bask in the sun's warmth, appreciate the starry nights along with the local people, admire the herds of animals wandering freely, contemplate the singing of multicolored birds, savor a ripened fruit freshly-gathered after months and perhaps years of toil, pray to the God rain, and receive his blessing through that miracle. All these things direct us immediately to God, as inseparable elements of our individual and communal prayers with the semi-desert's inhabitants. A fervent Samburu prayer, invoked almost always under the shade of a tree, often takes the following form: *Nkai, taa Nkai ai, taa Nkai ang, taa Nkai swom, mikinturraa, nimirikino, nimiking'uaa. Nkai ai incoo iyioo Nkare* ("O Lord, be my Lord, be our God, be the God of our herds, don't repulse me, don't abandon me. My Lord, give us water").

6) The desert, a place for decisions

In the solitude of the desert, Jesus engages in prayer with the Father. He overcomes temptation. He accepts baptism with the Spirit's strength. After his desert experience, Jesus began his sermon on the Kingdom of God (Lk. 4 :16-20; Mt. 4 :17). "Repent, for the kingdom of heaven is at hand."

His message changed the world, for it spoke with authority. The heart of Jesus' message is the Kingdom of God; he then chose the first disciples, to begin with them, his Church (Mt. 4 :18-22; Mk. 1 :16-20; Lk. 6 :12-16).

Strengthened by prayer and filled with the Holy Spirit, Jesus made his most important decisions: the announcement of the Kingdom up to its final days, and the founding of his Church.

150

Jesus invites us to be vigilant and to pray. Jesus prayed in the face of temptation. If at the present time even great entrepreneurs feel the need for silence, solitude and prayer in order to make important decisions, that is all the more reason why we should assume a constant attitude of prayer in our lives, so that we might bring our responsibilities to a happy conclusion, and fulfill the will of God.

The physical desert can be a great help; nevertheless, we must not forget that Jesus invited us to worship God in Spirit and in truth (Jn. 4 :23), "neither on this mountain nor in Jerusalem will you worship the Father" (Jn. 4 :21).

Places of worship must not always be closed areas or human construction. We can worship God anywhere, for we cannot imprison nor possess him.

When God visited them, Abraham, Moses, Samuel, Elijah, and Mary of Nazareth replied in the same way: "Here I am Lord" (1 Sam. 3 :4).

The Samburu people teach us with great simplicity to pray to Jesus and to praise Him in the tabernacle of the universe. Their council of elders always makes major decisions after praying to Nkai under the shade of a tree.

Before a meeting, a group of Samburu elders will pray in the following Manner: *Matang'asa Nkai pee kitum ataasisho* ("Let us permit God to guide us so that we may be able to do something").

7) The desert, a fulfilled life

It is in the desert, after temptation and tribulation, that the union of God and his people acquires its intensity, reality, substance and life.

After suffering temptation in the desert, Jesus emerges victorious, fulfilled, complete. He has placed his trust in the only savior possible, his Father. The love of the Father who has sent him, and the decision to live the love until its bitter end, find their fulfillment in Him.

Jesus' temptations in the desert give a new meaning and dimension to our own temptations. Jesus was tempted as we were, and for us. "Tested in everything, as were we" (Hb. 4 :15). If Christ has won, and emerged victorious, so, too, can we achieve victory. If Christ was tempted, it is not evil to be tempted. There are no shameful nor unconquerable temptations if we allow ourselves to be led by the Holy Spirit.

Jesus' temptations are the temptations of everyone. Jesus is the great leader who engenders assuredness and fulfillment. The disciples followed him because he bore witness, and spoke with authority. They saw in him the source of their fulfillment and happiness. Even in the midst of difficulties, Jesus was a completely happy man. "Where do you dwell?" they asked. Jesus replied, "Come and see" (Jn. 1 :35-51).

Everyone longs for happiness and fulfillment. The truth of the matter is human intelligence and the ability to do things rarely suffice as answers to their deep questioning and search for happiness.

For example:
Though we possess the means to live in fulfillment and to create a life of paradise, we are converting it into a living hell. We spend too much money on armaments, luxuries and vices.

Our bond with nature weakens by the day. Nature is wounded by vast irresponsible burning, the extinction of species, general pollution and senseless accumulation.

It is wonderful to learn about the bond between aborigines and nature that has endured for many years!

In order to solve our problems we almost always rely on the reason of strength, rather than on the strength of reason.

We confuse pleasure with happiness; we want to be happy, and many times, we are wretched; we are not happy with what we are. We live estranged by bread and circus. We profess one faith, and live another. We serve one God in the temple, and another in the street.

By his life and example, Jesus taught us the way to be happy, and to live the fullness of love in the company of the Creator.

One can notice the noble savage among the Samburu. In the midst of simplicity and need, suicide is never committed, as is the case in other cultures.

The local people pray to God-Nkai, asking him to grant them happiness. He is the source of all happiness and fulfillment. They constantly offer Nkai the following prayer: *Nkai ng'ora iyioo too nkonyek pokora are, tiningo iyioo too nkiyia, inco iyioo nikiomunu amu iyie nkitok alang ntoki pooki* ("God, look at us with your two eyes, listen to us with your ears, and grant us what we ask you for, for you alone are greater than all things").

8) The desert, a place to face our preaching

John preached in the desert, identifying himself in this way: "I am the voice of one crying in the desert; Make straight the way of the Lord, said the prophet Isaiah" (Jn. 1 :23). After his sermon, many were baptized. His mission gains strength; he refuses no one, but does require a personal commitment to justice.

The prophets who guided the people of Israel denounced their sins, proclaiming the goodness of Yahweh.

Although any area can become sacred, and suitable for a meeting with God, nevertheless, in the so-called "theological places," (holy places) where He reveals himself, it can be seen that poverty, humility, and simplicity usually surround the perception of the divine presence. It is understandable then, why one often says, "The poor are evangelizing us."

Jesus identifies with the poor. He came to give of none other than himself. Jesus came in order to love, not in order to triumph. The Messiah did not use his powers for personal reasons, to gain fame, riches, influence, or prestige; he came to show us God's mercy and great love for all human beings.

The Church's mission must identify with that of Jesus. We must leave our comfortable inner circles and go to the peripheral areas of the poor and marginalized. The great masses of poor and rejected do not figure in the present-day liberal market economy. They are non-productive. They are but a cry clamoring for justice, deserving of everyone's support.

What percentage of the Church's pastoral-care workers are in marginalized areas and urban slums? How many of the missionary communities labor in marginalized areas of primary evangelization? Can it be possible that many cities are over-staffed with pastoral workers and that the Church's bureaucracy has reached alarming numbers?

How many people are ready to leave the comfortable confines of their homes in order to share Jesus' mission with those who do not know him?

The Samburu pray to God in this way: *Nkai ai, miarie iyioo monko nikias te maddai ang'amu ikira nkerra naimina to nkop nalakua* ("My God, do not slay us for the foolish things we do out of pride, for we are but sheep, lost in a faraway place").

153

9) The desert, a life experience

If we have previously stated having experienced the desert as a place of death, we must now decidedly assert that it is, at the same time, one of life and new creation.

In the Bible, the desert is portrayed as related to life. It is identified with the combative era, of struggle and temptation, from which the Lord will emerge as defender of his people. In the desert, people learned to read the signs of the times and God's manifestations, through faith.

The great mystics lived their supernatural experience by undergoing what they referred to as passage through the images of "desert, dark night, and complete abandonment."

Jesus came to give us abundant life (Jn. 10 :10). He conquers temptation: "May this chalice pass from me, let it succeed with trust, let not my will be done, but yours". Filled with life, he gives life to all, curing also the lepers (Mk. 1 :45; Mt. 8 :2; Lk. 5 :12). He helps all of us to recover our dignity, to overcome enslavement and to live out our lives fully.

In Hosea, the desert recalls the place of "encounter" between God and his people (Hos. 2 :16). The desert represents the route of searching and freedom; it is the discovery of truth and fulfillment; it is silence and oasis; it quiets and awakens; the desert causes us to discover our vocation, making us people of God, who value life and the essential. The desert is radiant.

Our Primary Evangelization experience among this traditional tribe of Eastern Africa continually fills us with life. Our presence, constantly facing difficulties, doubts and even death itself, "is likened to the seed the man threw into the furrow. Many days and nights go by, during which he sleeps and awakens, while the seed germinates and grows, without his knowing why" (Mk. 4 :26). The Kingdom of God's seed is germinating among those who do not know Jesus. We, too, get to know him more deeply. The Holy Spirit accompanies us. He is life.

Our faith grows purer and stronger, the more we delve into the sacred terrain of this new culture. We receive through giving. The painful steps of introduction, inculturation, learning a new language, the loneliness associated with not being able to communicate, fear and anxiety facing something new, the initial rejection when, because we are poor, we cannot offer anything, all acquire new meaning.

154

God is present in this culture. The newness of Jesus and his Word, continue to find fertile territory among many people of good will. The Holy Spirit is our guide.

In the name of those who called us and sent us here, we denounce the incidences of death and injustice in this tribe: Governmental neglect, corruption among the few leaders, female mutilation through circumcision, discrimination and overworking of women, theft and other cultural practices that go against life.

The local people continue to discover in us - the mission team - something more than just outside advocates; they see in us signs of hope, solidarity in the face of suffering, guidance through difficulties, a reason for uniting, a means for rescuing their lives, and witnesses to the love of God-Nkai, through Jesus Christ.

The Samburu say: "*Kore te nemeatae Nkai meatae Itungani amu ninye Nkishon*" ("If there is no God, there are no people, for He is life").

We Yarumal Missionaries provide a health service there. We fight for life. Our vehicle is the regional ambulance and frequently we are called upon to transport the ill to the closest hospital. Wo have already had some of them die en route, and some babies have been born in our vehicle.

Part
FOUR

THE ORIGIN OF THE MISSION
FROM LATIN AMERICA

T he idea of a mission born in Latin America and inspired by theological principles renewed by Vatican Council II, presents clear evidence of originality going beyond subtleties and emphasis. The Puebla document No. 368, produced by the Latin American Conference of Bishops, proposes: "Our Churches can offer something original and important - their idea of salvation and liberation, the richness of their popular religiosity, the experience of ecclesiastic base communities, the flourishing ministries, and the expectations and joy of their faith. We have now realized missionary efforts that can be deepened and must be expanded."

A mission "arising from poverty"

When our Yarumal Missionaries arrived in the semi-desert, one of the most difficult tasks was to help the local people understand the idea of a poor mission. How could we move from dependency to dignified organization? Expecting much material help, some of them openly stated: "If you Colombians have nothing to give us, you may leave now. A poor man cannot lead another poor man."

The expression, "out of poverty," must be considered not only from a socio-economic point of view, but also by its theological, ascetic and paschal ramifications.

Latin American theology has found in the poor and in poverty - a theological area - the greatest support for its expansion. Salvation is a key act of liberation from all forms of servitude and oppression.

Poverty has become a source of inspiration for the new spirituality that places in relief the condition's paschal aspect. Latin America has been inspired by "poverty in general," and its own poverty, to commit its efforts to that end.

Human logic differs from the logic of Christ. In spite of the needs we have in Latin America, the poor are challenging the Church to "give out of poverty."

159

For this reason, the new type of mission they propose, does not bring, but uncovers; doesn't just give, but receives; does not conquer, but shares in the search. Missionaries should not be teachers, but apprentices of the truth, enriching themselves with all that is good and true in other people and other cultures. As a missionary in another culture, one can learn more than he can teach. "The poor evangelize us." The poor teach us to discover what is basic and important to life.

The Latin American mission, therefore, is:

1. A mission of "the poor to the poor"

Its uniqueness lies in being a Church of minor importance, both economically and politically. They are people who do not enjoy the power of decision making on the world stage.

We are a Church of marginalized people, oppressed and subject to the framework of injustice, but at the same time, made up of men and women who for years have experienced a profound faith in their lives, assimilating the values of generosity, forgiveness, and spiritual enrichment, through suffering and a supportive attitude which teaches us to share. For this reason we understand that poverty should not be viewed as a problem, but rather as a solution, or "quarry" of values. The evangelizing power of a poor person is one of the most moving and enriching discoveries of the Puebla Episcopal Conference.

A mission originating in Latin America, then, will divest itself of the idea of abundance. It will be a process of encounter with an indigent brother:
- Arising from our poverty.
- With meager means.
- For the poorest of the poor.
- In the manner of poor who can hope.
- Who are happy with simple things.
- And can trust in a power that does not emanate from themselves, but from God.

2. A mission of Church to Church

The mission is not conceived to be an activity of specific individuals or institutions. It becomes an entity committed to the entire Christian community. Missionary zeal is not charisma granted to certain people, but rather, something inherent to the nature of a Christian being, and to the nature of the Church itself. "The 'Church' does not have a mission - 'mission' has a Church." Missionary activity should be a reciprocal activity through which the giving Church also receives:
- The sphere for all members of a communal church is extended beyond normal boundaries.

160

- Sending out missionaries, a communal task, involves the entire church community with the mission.
- Fraternal relations with a distant Church may cause questioning in the local pastoral   mission and result in changes to the labor of evangelizing.
- Local missionary needs are discovered, prompting the establishment of programs in the parish communities.
- Vocations and ministries among local people increase.
- People returning to the service of the local pastoral mission make it more dynamic.

3. A mission of communion and participation

An original program arises here, called "sister Churches." It is a mission undertaken as a total ecclesiastical community effort, with emphasis on the aspect of brotherhood, where everyone reciprocates by contributing and receiving. A program of permanent interaction, it involves communication and the interchange of spiritual, material and pastoral aids.

4. A mission with a liberation awareness

One of the finest contributions of the Latin American brand of theology has been the emphasis placed on earthly salvation, as an integral part of the transcendence of eternal salvation.

Through the lucid evaluation of situations involving oppression and the marginality resulting from unjust organizations, the people of Latin America find their greatest hope in Jesus' Gospel. Here, they find a satisfactory way to struggle for justice and to overcome all impediments to adequate freedom.

A missionary setting out from Latin America has shared the suffering of his people through personal experience with hunger, chronic illness, illiteracy, wars, unemployment, impoverishment, injustice in international relations - and even more so in commercial exchange - as well as in political, economic and cultural situations related to neo-colonialism.

All of the suffering our people have experienced has brought us closer to, and solidified us with, our third-world brothers and sisters of Africa and Asia. A *southern - to- southern mission*.

Evangelization, then, is the process of introducing Jesus Christ, Liberator of humanity.

Liberation must be total; evangelization, essential.

5. A mission, not of conquest, but of introduction and testimony

The mission originating in Latin America is based on vivid testimony of Jesus Christ and his Kingdom, offering the richness of a simple, poor and humble religious experience, rather than the strength of a culture or a political power.

An American mission must also be free of all semblance of conquest, whether it be on a political, cultural or religious level.

It will not be a political type of conquest, since it is not a mission emanating from the center of power to an outlying area, but from periphery to periphery. It will not appear to be aligned with any political power, but will arrive without the semblance of strength, typified by it own weakness, and based on insubstantial means.

The mission from Latin America will not be one of cultural conquest.
Our Church is a community in search of its own identity, desirous of allowing other cultures to participate in this pursuit, while making each of them a place for the Gospel's manifestation; yet, remaining aware of the fact missionary activity must recognize and not violate the mysterious universal action God exercises over these cultures through the "seeds of the word," dispersed to all corners of the world.

Nor will it be a mission of spiritual conquest.
Characterized as a mission of introduction, the Latin American mission will not presume to be one of salvation. Though it is true that the Church and its emissaries offer the means to salvation, in the final analysis, salvation is exclusively the work of the Holy Spirit. In Latin America we have suffered all the consequences of these types of conquest, through our own flesh and blood. For this reason, our presence, enlightened by the Resurrection of Jesus Christ, must not create any doubt as to our motives in the minds of our brothers and sisters from other continents.

6. A mission that is not permanent, but itinerant
One of the characteristics a mission must have is mobility. That was Jesus' mandate, "Go throughout the world," and the apostles went from place to place. The missionary Church was itinerant; an emerging Church was responsible for the birth of another Church.

We Latin Americans learned a great deal about the first missionaries who went to our continent and decided to establish themselves permanently, hindering the expansion of nascent Latin American Churches, for lack of missionary intent.

That is why we believe in temporary missions. The missionary coming out of Latin America will stay in one area only as long as his presence is absolutely necessary, avoiding permanent reliance on outside help by the region's Christians.

It is also a good idea to distinguish clearly between *itinerancy* and *instability*. In Africa, for example, we have experienced helping communities grow in their faith. After several years, some communities have matured in the areas of ministry, vocations and finances. We missionaries have placed these areas in the hands of native workers, and gone to regions where the need is more acute, where Jesus Christ remains unknown. Our presence in these poor and marginal areas should not be perpetual. We are obliged to prepare the way for local laborers of Christ.

7. An inculturated mission

One of the great themes of today's theology is the inculturation of the faith. The Church is born, not transplanted. It puts down roots in the very culture of the people being evangelized. Thus, the Church is born in all corners of the earth. It is not a question of adapting the European Church to a certain people, by making a few modifications. The Church is born, not formulated. Establishing a Church is quite distinct, for it deals more with administration. The Church is born out of presentation of the Word, and arrives at faith. And faith leads to the Sacrament of regeneration. The Church is born when the Gospel of conversion penetrates cultural roots and transforms "mental judgments," decisive values, points of interest, trains of thought, sources of inspiration, life patterns for humanity, (Encyclical No.19, "The Preaching of the Gospel," by Pope Paul VI).

We missionaries must struggle so that the Church of Jesus Christ in Africa is African; in Asia, Asian; and in America, American. The Church is but one, but with different manifestations in its fortuitous aspects. Unity in diversity is a sign of richness. Jesus' entire Church cannot be Romanized. The inculturation of the Gospel is one of the most polemic and interesting aspects of the Church.

From Latin America we are called forth to avoid manners of evangelization which violate the dignity of people or their cultures. We have noticed, many times, being forced to pay the consequences of a pattern of evangelization based on dependency and paternalism, or taken from European and North American models.

One of our colleagues in the semi-desert experienced why the elders chose to stop participating in religious celebrations. "If we can no longer receive blankets, food, tobacco, and medicine for our animals, then why do we come to Church?" they asked. The missionary's reply was, "If you come just to receive things, and not for the purpose of getting to know Jesus Christ and his Word, you may all leave. I did not come here to buy the people's faith." Even today, many yearn for former times. The younger generations have understood and are helping the older people. The new Christians are a beacon for the people. Faith is similar to a bonfire; if it is covered, it will go out.

A new kind of well-defined Church:

- The universal mission is to assess poverty from an evangelical point of view, and to discover its paschal meaning in order to introduce the Gospel from within that condition.

- A well-defined mission Church is one that has awakened from the lethargy and routine to which it became accustomed after many centuries of receiving, without feeling obliged to give in return.

- It is, just the same, a Church that, faced with the great problems of the universal mission, minimizes its own problems.

- A Church faithful to the teachings of the Gospel, becomes dynamic from day to day, because the command to go "above and beyond," invites it to rise out of stagnation.

- This Church understands its obligation, more than "keeping" the faith, is to give it to those who do not know it.

- And finally, the aforementioned universal missionary plan helps diocesan bishops to regain their pastoral identity, as successors to the apostles and representatives of the only Shepherd who has "other sheep who are not of this fold" (Jn. 10 :16). They cannot, then, be content to minister to the one "sheep" in the fold and forget the ninety-nine who are distanced. During our experience as priests associated with the Yarumal Missionaries in Kenya, we were visited by two Colombian bishops, Monsignor Darío Monsalve and Monsignor Gustavo Martínez Frías, both of whom witnessed the testimony of their priests at the mission, far removed from the borders of their original dioceses.

A new kind of Mission:

Finally, we may conclude that the missionary thrust of our continent proposes a new type of mission, leaving behind the old theological and pastoral programs of previous centuries. The changes are:

- From being a mission that only gives or only receives to a mission of encounter and interchange.

- From a mission belonging to missionary institutions to a mission of a well-defined Church.

- From a mission which baptizes individuals to a mission baptizing cultures in depth.

- From a mission of Christianity to a mission of small Christian communities.

- From a clerical mission to a mission of all of God's people.

- From a mission whose sole objective is the Church to a mission whose end is the Kingdom of God.

- From a mission pertaining to a specific geographic entity to a mission of introduction to groups of people scattered here and there.

- From a mission underwritten by some Churches to a mission which is the task of all Churches.

- From an assistance-providing mission to a mission promoting justice and inherent freedom.

- From a mission for the poor to a mission run by the poor.

- From a mission protected by civil authority to a mission without special privileges.

- From a mission built on the superiority of those who are knowledgeable to a mission arising from evangelical simplicity.

- From a stationary mission adhering to routine to an itinerant, imaginative mission.

- From a mission based on activities to a mission where prayer and contemplation are more important.

- From a mission of ideologies to a mission of testimony.

- From a mission that expends itself in pursuit of converts to a mission that creates a Christian community out of the dynamism of Primary Evangelization.

A new kind of diocesan priesthood:

The missionary commitment of the Latin American Church opens to the diocesan priest the possibility of fulfilling a "temporary" period of service beyond its borders. Such an experience represents a powerful element of pastoral and spiritual enrichment for him, as well as for his Church of origin. The diocesan priest needs to free himself from the tiring effects of a routine, simplistic pastoral charge, and to pursue the broader horizons offered by the universal mission. In this way, he recaptures the universal scope of his priestly mission, by looking beyond the narrow confines of his parish and his diocese.

For more than a decade, we Missionaries of Yarumal have witnessed this mutual enrichment by sharing the mission with diocesan priests associated with our Institute for a period of time. During my stay in Kenya, I was able to share my life with priests coming from the diocese of Ipiales and the Archdiocese of Medellín, both in Colombia.

Father Carlos Alberto Calderón chats with two young Samburu warriors. Nothing new happens in the pastoral world. Because everything is new! Happiness and joy do not come from the extraordinary, nor do possessions produce these feelings. They come from fascination with the commonplace.

Monsignor Gustavo Martínez, Colombian bishop, accompanied by the diocesan priests Eduardo Yepes and Edison Vela, being received by a Samburu family.

Among the Samburu, the celebration of a baptism with water and milk, called an nkarrer, has deep meaning, an effort to inculturate the Gospel.

WHY I AM GOING TO AFRICA
A farewell letter by Father Carlos Alberto

"Therefore let us also, having such a cloud of witnesses over us, ...run with patience to the fight set before us; looking toward the author and finisher of faith, Jesus".
(Hebrews 12 :1-2)

My dear Friends:

Many of you have already heard of my decision to go to Africa for several years, to work on a missionary project; others will find out from this letter to everyone. As I have done at other times in my life, I now also want to share the history and reason for this decision, which I do with a special greeting, full of affection for all of you.

Since becoming an ordained priest more than twenty years ago, I thought about the possibility of spending a few years of my life serving in a country or Diocese that is more marginal or more needy than my own Diocese of Medellín where I was ordained.

This plan never materialized, partly because one begins to settle down in his pastoral charge and becomes sort of rooted in his own city; perhaps our regionalist mentality also contributes to this; and in part because one becomes blind to the reading of signs and callings from that God who goes around murmuring "Good News" in history itself, and in daily happenings. Some of you are aware of my decision of a few years ago to go and work in the Diocese of Sincelejo, also mission territory here in our country; but this decision was based on other reasons and became quite an exit from and answer to a rather difficult religious assignment I held in those days. Even though it was a very enriching time in my ministerial life, it was not the realization of the plan I had dreamed of at the dawning of my priestly career.

Around the beginning of last May, purely by chance (today, I see it as more out of faith than by chance, as a divine voice, or true *Kairos*), I found out about the pastoral emergency in the program with which the missionaries of Yarumal and the diocesan priests were involved - a daring and refreshing project for the local Churches in view of Vatican II - based on the impossibility of two priests from the Archdiocese of Cali going to Kenya, as was planned. This produced in me an immediate and surprisingly happy reaction; it was a desire I held from the time of ordination.

It was so obvious and so clear to me, that without thinking about it twice, and moreover, without consulting any one - only after praying about it for a while - I decided to ask his excellency the Archbishop to consider the idea. The pastoral wisdom and reliability of Monsignor Héctor Rueda, our archbishop, was enough to place the decision in his hands. This time, it was clear to me, moreover, that it was not a question of asking for canonical permission to solve a personal problem or requesting authorization in order to experience an adventure, the product of a possible "missionary romanticism"; it was, rather, petitioning my bishop to send me to live the passion, through Jesus, through the Gospel, and through the poor, on the African continent, in a Church forging ahead on the road to faith, but poor and lacking pastoral resources; I would be taking part in an evangelization project which, without violating the culture and spirituality of those peoples, would introduce the newness of the Gospel; I would also be sharing life and the faith with the peoples of Africa, striving not to repeat among them what some Spaniards did some five-hundred years ago to our "Amer-India."

This opportunity, along with the pastoral generosity of His Excellency the Archbishop and his auxiliary bishops, made it possible, then, for me to undertake this new uprooting in my life and go to Kenya. This is a little bit of the decision's history, but I also want to share with you a feeling for what it means to me.

Going to Africa does not mean, primarily, going to be a missionary; as if I had not been one already! It was just that the mission would now be over there in Africa, or another continent outside of our own. I am convinced that anyone who has not lived his faith, his Christian life, and his ministry in a missionary way (that is to say, permanently embodying the Good News of the Gospel, and spreading it), is not qualified nor empowered to go to Africa or any other part of the world as a missionary. Thanks to God, my theological training was nourished, and continues to be, by the Church doctrine of Vatican II, and by the ecclesiastical teachings of Medellín's 1968 Episcopal Conference. From that time on, I have been able to discover that a Church, not missionary in scope, is not Jesus Christ's Church; and a Christian who is not a missionary, is not a follower of Jesus. Evangelization is an essential mark of the Church and we have been especially reminded of this by Vatican II, as well as by the actions of the Latin American Church in recent decades. What is happening is that perhaps we have not taken seriously the Council's energizing ecclesiology that tells us the Church has a reason for being only if it

168

becomes an historic Diakon of salvation and liberation, or endeavor to serve mankind.

I am not going to Africa, though, because I feel that there is nothing to be done here, that there is no pressing missionary work here or in any other corner of the globe where we may be called to live out the evangelization of our faith. Going to Africa (It could have been to anywhere else!) is nothing more than changing milieu for spreading the Gospel; it is nothing greater than the opportunity to share my zeal for Jesus Christ and for the Gospel, with a more ministerially vulnerable Church than ours; it also means being aware of the Gospel's universality, so apparent in Jesus' preaching and in His sending forth the disciples (Mt. 28 :16-20; Lk. 10 :1-16).

A second feeling I have discovered based on this decision, and which I also wish to share with you, is that I am convinced I am going to Africa not because I am the best and most committed of the Archdiocese's priests; on the contrary! As any Christian, I also need to be converted, disestablish myself, and become more like Jesus, etc...Over there in Kenya, I could become a poorer servant of His than those of you who remain behind; and I have to be careful of that. It doesn't mean that those of us who go to a mission "Ad Gentes" (to the people), are the truest Christians or the most committed priests; in my opinion this is crystal clear; the authenticity, propheticalness, and testimony of a Christian life is the result of living faithfully Christ's Teachings wherever we may be, where God's Spirit inspires us to be; the Church would be quite different if all of us members who choose to follow Jesus, would do so seriously, intensely; if we were a little more human in our relationships, more in solidarity with the weak and suffering, less complicated in our manner of being and mixing with others, struggle harder for justice, more contemplative, more fraternal, less arrogant, less money-hungry, less destructive of life and nature, and less ambitious for power.

All of you here, as well as those of us who for a period of time enter other Churches, have the duty and the great responsibility to be more faithful to the Gospel, to be more passionate about making others happy, especially the poorest of the poor and the weakest, as Jesus did. From this perspective, everything that has arisen based on the assertions of some of my male and female friends has also become very clear to me and gives meaning to my decision. They have said, "How is it possible that you are leaving right at the time when you are receiving great recognition on an ecclesiastic as well as civil level? Now precisely when you are enjoying your finest moment?"

And exactly because of such statements, the decision has given me a great feeling of peace. It has also been very helpful to listen to Jesus's admonition to his disciples: Woe to you when all men speak well of you! (Lk. 6 :26); likewise, John the Baptist's reply to his followers based on the cry they directed to him before beginning Jesus' mission: "It is necessary that he grow, and I diminish" (Lk. 3 :25-30).

A third meaning I have discovered lately is that such surprises from the Holy Spirit (my interpretation of this decision) are deeply invigorating and renewing experiences. When I made the decision, already a few months past, I didn't perceive it to be like this. Little by little, as I have begun to share the decision with many of you I have felt a fascinating inner rejuvenation; I have felt a sense of happiness like very few times in my life; I am sharing this with deep humility and frankness; this is the happiness that is experienced as one delves deeper into a relationship with God; I feel that this decision is making me sense the love and tenderness of God more intensely, and the result is happiness; it is like a gift and a commitment at the same time.

At present, while delving deeper into this, I became more aware of the need to depart for Africa without any hero or martyr complex, but rather, with a clear understanding of my limitations, and with a vast openess to learning the Gospel of Africa, with a great desire to uncover the "seeds of the Word," that are in those African cultures, and respecting them, not repeating (as I have previously stated) what some of our European brothers did to our Amerindian cultures, and what many Europeans have done until recently to African peoples. Finally, I am going away very happy, though with a certain fear and trepidation, but yes, quite convinced that whoever is calling me, will be there in many forms, one of which will be through all of you, your company, friendship, your prayers and fraternal support.

I also hope to arrive in Africa barefoot, and with my backpack filled with the Gospel and a great desire to give of myself. I must also add that I have felt strongly my entire family's support, and their presence in my mother's spirit; I must not forget to say that they were one of my greatest worries in making this decision, due to the deep void in their lives caused by my mother's recent death. But as in many other moments of my life, they have shown great generosity and boundless support. The generosity of my brothers and sisters and the support of so many male and female friends are my best passport to Africa.

In conclusion, I would like to give you an idea of my itinerary: Toward the end of August, I will travel to London where I will attend an intensive refresher course in English, one of Kenya's national languages. Then, around the end of October I will go to Nairobi to have my first contact with the culture and the country itself and begin the study of Kiswahili, another of Kenya's national languages. There, I will be part of the Missionaries of Yarumal team, and then will be sent to work in a diocese with the most urgent needs. From there, I will write to you again! I am counting on all of you for your friendship, support and prayers.

All my love, Carlos Alberto Calderón.

170

With shaven heads, the women roam the region amid songs, dances and prayers. The water has returned and the people celebrate the rain festival.

The drought has been severe. The women danced, praying to Nkai and the child was given the name of Jesus. He will be a shepherd and warrior, and will teach his tribe to know the God and Father of all tribes and cultures.

AFRICA IN MY HEART

"Africa is a staved symphony of a thousand drums, cries, sorrows, quiet, dreams and hopes. Blended together there, as in a *chiaroscuro*, are the verdency of the mountains and the reddish desert, weather-beaten skin and hearts made gentle, a diversity of ethnic groups and multiple languages, harmoniously conjoined by a common root. In Africa, I have learned to love in this environment of plurality and diversity, divesting my heart and my mind of all prejudice. There, I have experienced love and a warm welcome."

In Africa, I have felt the human kindliness of the poor and the tenderness of God-Nkai, the Father of all tribes and cultures. I dream that the desert is blooming while numerous men and women, invigorated by the Holy Spirit, spread the seeds of good-will, kindness, solidarity, peace, love and life. I dream that the white and the black person embrace fraternally, and united, follow the Good Shepherd of Nazareth.

I dream that "love conquers the myth of distance," and that one day, either in the desert or the boundless plain, in communion with God, humans, and nature, I shall return to the **Great Beginning**, though my body may become food for the hyenas or converted to sand in the deep, immense desert.

The seduction of Africa is eternal.

J.I.F.

171

YARUMAL MISSIONERS

Calle 55 No. 45-44 Medellín, Colombia
Telephone: (57-4) 513 13 32 - 513 13 27
Fax: (57-4) 251 99 43
A.A. 3309 Medellín, Colombia
E-mail: imeymed@epm.net.co
www.catholic-forum.com/proyectos/mxy

Orders:

Jorge Iván Fernández
YARUMAL MISSIONERS
2317 Washington Ave.
Bronx, NY 10458
Telephone: (718) 561 82 48
Fax: (718) 562 25 21
New York, USA.
E-mail: imeyusa1@aol.com

Telephone: (57-4) 234 72 45
513 67 15 - 511 20 78
Fax: (57-4) 413 63 98
Medellín, Colombia.